"It takes courage, fortitude and faith to navigate the deep waters of loss and grief. Major Brian Saunders has provided us not a roadmap, but an authentic first-hand description of a father and son journey during and following the loss of the dearly beloved woman of their lives. This is not a candy-coated tale or a how-to book, but rather a story that will move, challenge and bless the reader because of the profound struggles and victories of an ongoing saga of life and loss."

JACK ANDERSON, Ph.D.
Director, Officer Care & Development
USA Western Territory

"*Losing Leticia* by Major Brian Saunders, a Salvation Army officer and pastor, tells a true story of the author and his son's confrontation with the death of a wife and mother. It's a positive, loving, and honest book that examines the mother's losing fight for life and the father's fight through grief and, finally, achievement of equilibrium.

A series of Salvation Army bulletins through 2009, included in the book, kept Leticia's friends and colleagues informed of her declining health. She was admitted to the hospital for the last time in August 2009 after having a stroke. Four months later, on December 14, 2009, Leticia died at age 47. She had stayed the course and fought a good fight. She was secure in her faith.

Brian dealt with his own feelings primarily with letters to and from two very close friends, Craig and Ivan. The book also includes these letters, sources of unburdening and value for Brian. C.S. Lewis' book, *A Grief Observed*, written following the death of his own wife, became another "helping friend" through the shock involved in Brian's processing of Leticia's death. The book is quoted often. In his preface, Brian wrote: 'Lewis never found answers, but he did find peace.' Then he adds: 'My prayer is that we will find it, too.'

The stages of grief do not have any rigid order, and often rotate in a mixed fashion. Using slightly different names for feelings, Brian rotated through them in a wonderful openness

In moving through the 'dark valley' Brian spent much time with Psalm 23. Even as he concludes his book, he recognizes Leticia 'will always be part of us,' writing: *even though I walk through the darkest valley, I will fear no evil, for you are with me* (Psalm 23:4).

Writing this book has facilitated his movement though grief, not its ending. The reader will learn much about feelings and thoughts, grieving and loss."

ROBERT DOCTER, Ph.D., O.F.
Founding Editor, New Frontier Publications
USA Western Territory

"I've always been intrigued by the Peanuts comic strip comment, 'Good Grief, Charlie Brown.' Here, in *Losing Leticia: A Husband's Journey Through the Valley of Shadow,* we come to better understand how the deep grief of losing a loved one can move toward deep good. We are at a loss with Leticia's promotion to Glory, but we are at a distinct advantage with Major Brian Saunders' recollections and revelations about his journey. The valley, after all, is where the flowers bloom and living water flows. That's good. So is this book."

JAMES KNAGGS, COMMISSIONER
Territorial Commander
USA Western Territory

"Few things are as private as grief. Because each grieves in his own way, most people never find the words to describe the steps on their path of bereavement. Brian Saunders, however, has managed to take us into his head and into his heart. This is largely done by sharing the emails written back and forth with his two best friends, from whom he withheld no expression of his sorrow. Not only is his book touching and compelling to read, it is, in a sense, a resource. Those who grieve will find it cathartic. Those who wish to comfort the grieving will find themselves guided by this honest look at the angst of losing a loved one. And all who read it will be reminded that no measure of misery and loneliness that life brings can overcome the ultimate victory found in relationship with Christ."

AMY REARDON, MAJOR
Corps Officer, Seattle Temple
USA Western Territory

"This book moves me in a special way. Major Brian Saunders opens his heart to let us glimpse the poignancy of his experience in coping with the early death of his wife, Leticia. Readers who have walked a similar path will be blessed, but so too will those who have yet to know the awful pain of such a loss. The book is grounded in a Christian outlook, but the author does not pretend that faith in the face of death is easy. Wholeheartedly, I commend this sensitive, thoughtful, and revealing volume to readers everywhere."

GENERAL SHAW CLIFTON (RET.)
International Leader of The Salvation Army, April 2006-2011

"Major Brian Saunders has written both an inspirational and transparent account of God's love in action in the life of Leticia Saunders, his beloved wife who was promoted to Glory in 2009. The reader will soon discover that Brian and Leticia were clearly bound by an unusually deeply shared commitment to God and abiding devotion to one another. I had the privilege of serving alongside Leticia as a fellow Salvation Army officer for more than 20 years. She was one of the most intelligent, creative, and nurturing people I have ever known. Leticia was also a woman of great courage, even as she suffered great physical trials. Through the best and worst of times, Leticia was blessed to have a husband who remained faithful and loyal. Above all, Brian was able to see God's hand at work in every step of the journey that Leticia and Brian and their son Holden would travel together.

I suspect that few of us would fully emerge from the shadow of shared suffering with the love of our life. However, I know that Leticia's legacy of faith and wisdom has been a source of abounding joy and comfort to Brian and to those who reflect on her contribution to their own lives. I am confident that this book will be a great blessing to all its readers, particularly those who today are passing through the valley of shadow. Blessedly, it has been that journey that has set the stage for Brian's present ascension to vibrant faith and perfect peace."

EDWARD HILL, LT. COLONEL
Chief Secretary
Singapore, Malaysia and Myanmar Territory

"Grief is a fact of life. Whether we experience it firsthand or walk through it with someone else, all of us have to deal with the pain of losing someone. Piercingly personal and authentic, Major Brian Saunders traces the steps of his own journey through this valley of shadow we call grief. He exposes his soul as he asks the questions we all ask: 'Why did you let this happen God; what good can possibly come of this?' Brian pulls no punches as he challenges God and seeks to find restoration and meaning. Yet he also demonstrates a faith and assurance in God. The underlining message is that God is always there; always here. The journey is long, he reminds us, but he is never alone. As a psychologist, teacher and Christian, I highly recommend this book to anyone who has experienced loss or who helps others through their loss."

ARCHIBALD D. HART, M.SC., PH.D.
Senior Professor of Psychology and Dean Emeritus,
Graduate School of Psychology,
Fuller Theological Seminary

"Major Brian Saunders shares from his heart about an experience no one wants to go through. He and Holden have shown how they have walked with God and totally relied on him in this time of loss and grieving. We were fortunate to know Leticia and saw her incredible love for Brian and Holden, and her passion for ministry. By sharing this account, Brian honors Leticia's life and ministry long after her promotion to Glory and reaffirms that God is in control even through very difficult circumstances."

STEVE AND MARCIA SMITH, LT. COLONELS
Secretary for Personnel and Community Care Ministries/VAVS/Older
Adult Ministries and Women's Auxiliaries Secretary, respectively
USA Western Territory

Losing Leticia

A husband's journey in the
valley of the shadow

By Brian Saunders

Losing Leticia
A husband's journey in the valley of shadow
Brian Saunders
2016 Frontier Press

Scripture quotations are from THE HOLY BIBLE, NEW INTERNATIONAL VERSION®, NIV®
Copyright © 1973, 1978, 1984, 2011 by Biblica, Inc.® Used by permission.
All rights reserved worldwide.

Saunders, Brian
Losing Leticia

December 2016

ISBN 978-0-9968473-3-9
Printed in the United States

FRONTIER PRESS
THE SALVATION ARMY USA WESTERN TERRITORY

FOREWORD

By Dave Hudson, Colonel

BRIAN SAUNDERS OPENS THIS BOOK by saying that it's "not for you." It is a memoir in which he tells his story, taking us through his wife Leticia's illness and death and the years that follow as he tries to reshape a life in the "valley of the shadow of death" for him and his son, Holden. Ironically, in the intimacy of its detail, his story becomes universal—a story of grief to which we all can relate.

I have known Brian for many years. He began training to be an officer in The Salvation Army while I served as a divisional youth secretary. I often feel, as an officer who moves around often, that I have a thousand acquaintances and a few close friends. Yet Brian and I have a close mentor to mentee, uncle to nephew kind of relationship, and reading this book was like reading a story that I had lived.

Brian often quotes from and identifies with another famous Christian memoir writer, C.S. Lewis, who wrote *A Grief*

Observed after the death of his wife, Joy. Like Lewis, Brian never loses his faith, but he rails at God, not understanding why Leticia should be taken from him. Like Lewis, he struggles with truths he has always accepted, such as that "in all things God works for the good for those who love him" (Romans 8:28). And like Lewis, he wrestles with his own eschatological understanding, asking questions like, "Where is she now?"

I think it's the why questions that never do make sense. I remember asking God why, too. Why now? Why these people? I know in my head that God uses all things for his glory, but it didn't seem to reconcile with my heart.

Unlike Lewis, Brian does not walk in the valley of the shadow of death alone. He has a teenage son, Holden, and a sacred charge from Leticia to bring him through to adulthood as a man of faith. Over the years, through intimate father-and-son moments, we watch that happen.

Brian also has two close friends with whom he shares everything. Their exchanges, through emails, provide a close-up look at the importance, particularly for men, of having deep relationships. This becomes a story within the story.

This memoir will also resonate particularly with Salvation Army officers. The final days of Leticia's illness happens during a busy Christmas season when they are corps officers in Hawaii. They try to keep up with all of their responsibilities as her condition worsens, until the corps "ohana" (family) grieves with Brian and takes on the burden of the corps work. When Brian is given "farewell orders" from the place where he feels secure and where there are so many memories of his wife, he and Holden have a hard time with the idea of leaving. Then, in his new appointment, God shows him that Leticia is there too. He finds that her legacy will continue, as he applies lessons he has learned from her about being an officer and as young women she has influenced take their own place in the Army.

My favorite type of movie is predictable, ends happy and makes you feel good. This is not the way I would have written the script for Brian or Leticia, but it does put flesh and bone to things that sometimes feel theoretical. This grief reveals pain in a way that makes faith be faith because it's out of our control. In one of Leticia's last public testimonies, she said that she had learned that it's OK to not be OK. That's a lesson we all need to learn—that things in our stories are perhaps not what we want or the best we could hope for, but that's OK.

Ultimately, Brian's memoir is about finding peace with God in a time of deep struggle. He might be in the valley, along with others of us who are in our own valleys, but he knows who is beside him—and so can you. That's a powerful lesson for us all.

PREFACE

Dear Reader,

The first thing you need to know is that this book is not for you. It's for me. It began as a collection of reports, letters, and journals. The reports kept friends informed of the progress and prognosis of my wife, Leticia, while she was in the hospital. The letters were to a couple of very close friends I've known since I was a kid, Craig Bowler and Ivan Wild—conversations over a virtual cup of coffee. When I needed to share with someone after Leticia's death, I naturally turned to them. The journals were my way of clearing out my heart, time and again, as it threatened to break with emotion in the months and years following Leticia's death.

So this writing is for me. It has been my release valve, my therapy. It's in your hands now as a witness to one family's journey through the valley of grief. It's a collection of memories, feelings, thoughts, and ideas. It traces my journey through this valley—first with Leticia, then alone, with my son.

A Grief Observed is C.S. Lewis's memoir of the weeks immediately following his wife's death due to cancer. Lewis railed against God, accused Him of cruelty, questioned His providence. He lashed out at those who offered well-meaning but thoughtless clichés, and he considered deeply his own eschatological theology. My feelings in the months following Leticia's death mirror many of the sentiments expressed by Lewis after his wife's death. How could a loving God do this? Why did He take her? Where exactly is she? Lewis asked the same questions we all might ask. And, like us, he got no answer. God did not speak words of explanation or comfort. God did not offer reason or justification.

Lewis did not find the answers he was looking for. He did, however, find peace. He came to terms with his grief, with his questions, and with his God. Through the agonizing passions of loss came a deeper understanding of life and death, faith and trust. He saw a bigger God—a God who still cared, a God who still held this ranting, doubting, dismissive child in the palm of His hand. So maybe this book is not just for me. Maybe it's for any one of us who has lost a loved one—perhaps you. Lewis never found answers, but he did find peace. My prayer is that we will find it too.

May God bless you!

Brian

CONTENTS

PROLOGUE

Dear Ivan & Craig,

I had the dream again last night. It was the same as always: the path, the valley, the darkness. I'm walking along this path alone as it enters a valley. The path meanders through different landscapes—sometimes thick with trees; other times, barren as a desert. Sometimes the path goes through a chasm, with walls of rock on both sides. Then it flattens out and enters a meadow, with dandelions and lilacs carpeting the landscape. A gentle stream gurgles to one side, sometimes disappearing into the brush or seeming to dry up completely, but it always comes back. The path is there, but I cannot always see it as I press forward through the darkness. Sometimes there are lights—lanterns along the rock walls or moonglow shining from above. At other times, the path grows very dark—the lights fade away and I am left stumbling in inky blackness that presses in on me from all sides.

Somehow, I know I will be on this path the rest of my life. This is a permanent journey, a walk that will never cease. It's a trail that I must travel; there is no choice. I am on it now, and it's a long, long road. So I make my way—sometimes with purpose; other times, wandering aimlessly. Sometimes it feels as if I am being led—like someone unseen is walking alongside. Other times, I press on without a guide, completely alone. Yet there is peace and encouragement. I'm alone, yet I know I am not alone. It is dark, yet I know that the light will come again.

Walking together

> **"**
>
> I readily admit to being smitten
>
> with her from our very
>
> first meeting. It was not long
>
> before romance blossomed.
>
> **"**

ONE

LETICIA AND I MET ON THE FIRST DAY OF SCHOOL at the Salvation Army's College for Officer Training in Rancho Palos Verdes, California, where we were both enrolled as cadets (students), preparing to become officers and ministers of the Gospel. I readily admit to being smitten with her from our very first meeting. It was not long before romance blossomed. We were married in 1991 and began our ministry as officers. We were a normal couple, experiencing the normal ups and downs of life together, figuring out how to balance work and family, and learning to accept each other for who we were and not who we wanted the other to be. Normal people. I liked it that way.

Born in 1962, Leticia was five years my senior. She often joked that she collected illnesses like other people collected souvenirs. As a pre-teen, she developed Osgood–Schlatter disease, which affects the knees of young people, particularly those involved in sports. She was diagnosed with lupus, an immune system disorder, when she was 14. She developed juvenile diabetes at 16; she missed her high school graduation because she was in a diabetic coma. I recall one conversation with clarity: It was before we became engaged, but during that period when we both knew we were heading toward marriage. Leticia sat me down and listed all her medical conditions and possible prognoses. She was blunt and honest; she wanted me to know what I was getting myself into. In my typical, optimistic (Leticia would say naïve) way, I simply dismissed her concerns, saying we would deal with it all as it came. To say that I did not know what I was getting into is quite the understatement.

By the time we were married, Leticia was taking four insulin shots a day, plus meal "boluses" to help cover in–between times. Still, no one would describe her as sickly. In fact, few people knew that she had any health issues at all. Despite the need to continually check her blood sugar levels and carefully monitor her diet and exercise, she continued to live an active, busy life, with no limitations whatsoever.

In 1995 our son Holden was born—two months premature and after a considerably difficult pregnancy, but healthy and whole. The pregnancy did some damage to Leticia's kidneys, however, and we were warned that her kidney function would have to be monitored carefully. Four years later, while we were living in England, Leticia contracted meningitis and spent two weeks in the hospital. Her doctor reported that her kidneys had suffered further damage but were still functioning at acceptable levels. Soon, however, the rate of deterioration began to accelerate.

Two years later, when we were back in Southern California, tests revealed that Leticia's kidneys were failing and that a transplant would eventually be needed. We had brought Holden with us that day, and he sat between Leticia and me as the doctor explained the types of transplants, the complexities of finding a match, and the lengthy process ahead of us. Holden, a precocious 8–year–old, quipped, "Try my dad; he'll do it." The doctor patiently explained that it was not quite that easy—that the donor and the patient needed to be a blood and tissue match, and that, although we were Mom and Dad, we were not related by blood. In fact, we were not even the same ethnicity, Letitia being of Latino ancestry. The odds against Mom and Dad being a match were astronomical—something like 30 million to one. I remember looking at Leticia, then Holden, and saying simply, "Test me."

God certainly has a sense of humor. Despite the odds, we were a match. The one person out of 30 million who could give Leticia a kidney was already living under the same roof with her. God's providence indeed! After almost six months of tests and preparations, our transplant was performed on October 7, 2003. Although Leticia now had to take numerous immunosuppressive medications, she was healthy once again.

In the years preceding the transplant, Leticia and I had occasionally discussed retirement. I wanted to retire to a condo somewhere near a beach; Leticia wanted a cabin in the woods. By the end of the conversation, however, she would always remind me that her opinion didn't really matter because the odds of her surviving past retirement age were very low. She wasn't being morbid or fatalistic, just realistic: the life expectancy of someone with severe diabetes is considerably less than that of a healthy person. But suddenly, with the transplant, the game had changed. I enjoyed telling her that the odds were now in her favor; she would have to decide on a retirement location after all!

Over the next few years we carried on with our busy ministry. We had postings as far afield as the United Kingdom and Guam as well as in our home territory, USA West, in California, Oregon, and Hawaii. Our responsibilities became increasingly complex as well as more physically, intellectually, and emotionally challenging. Leticia remained fairly healthy, although with the immunosuppressants weakening her immune system, she got sick a bit more frequently and seemed to take longer to recover from routine illnesses.

In the fall of 2008, while we were corps officers (pastors) in Honolulu, Leticia contracted celiac disease. Like lupus and diabetes, celiac is an auto–immune disease, with symptoms and damage mostly related to the digestive system. For Leticia, this was just another fact of life, no different from having diabetes. As a diabetic, she was already very careful with what she ate; now she became even more so. We learned to read labels carefully, shopped for gluten–free foods, created a "gluten–free" zone in the kitchen, and even bought separate toasters so no wheat crumbs would get near her gluten–free bread. The doctors assured us that as long as she continued with the gluten–free diet, she would be fine. Once again, we made the adjustment in our lives and moved on. Leticia accepted the change as just another hurdle to jump. I, ever the practical, naïve one, simply trusted that all would be well.

The immunosuppressants had caused considerable bloating, so we did not see it at first. Eventually, however, we noticed that she was losing weight. The doctors said that was to be expected with the change in diet, but the loss continued past what would be considered the plateau weight for someone with celiac. Leticia was militant with her diet, not allowing a micron of gluten anywhere near her. Still, the weight loss and accompanying dehydration and general weakness continued. The doctors were stumped. By June 2009, Leticia weighed 96 pounds.

The shadow falls

"

Needless to say, I was petrified.

My worst fears were being realized.

I remember feeling helpless,

scared, and unsure of what to do

or even how to pray.

"

TWO

THE SALVATION ARMY is a closeknit community. When someone is ill, the news is posted on message boards that officers and employees can read. I've included some of those bulletins—many of which I wrote. People would write to me and tell me how blessed they were to hear of Leticia's witness and testimony, and how they continued to pray for her and Holden and me.

BULLETIN
June 29, 2009

We have been informed that **Major Leticia Saunders**, Kauluwela Mission Corps, Honolulu, has been admitted to the hospital due to complications from Celiac Disease. Please keep her and the family in your prayers.

Finally, in late June, Leticia went into the hospital for some more concentrated testing and to get rehydrated. After several days of around–the–clock tests, she was diagnosed with Refractory Sprue—a rare form of celiac that does not respond to the typical gluten–free treatment. She would have to take supplements and some additional nutrients and fluids, but she would be OK. Doctors assured us that she would be able to adapt and normal life would resume. It did not work out that way.

BULLETIN
July 8, 2009

We have been informed that **Major Leticia Saunders** has been admitted to Straub hospital in Honolulu. She is in ICU due to kidney complications and pneumonia. Doctors continue to test for further infections on her lungs. Brian reports that her kidney function is back to normal and that she will remain in the hospital for another few days. Please continue to pray for Leticia and the family.

Just another hurdle, we thought. After two weeks the doctors felt that Leticia was well enough to return home. This turned out to be easier said than done. She had been pumped full of so much fluid that she was extremely bloated, weighing almost twice as much as when she entered the hospital. She was still weak and, in her condition, virtually incapable of getting around on her own. Holden was to start high school that week. Apart from taking him to and from school, I stayed home with Leticia, acting as nurse and helper. Then the world fell out from under us.

BULLETIN
August 4, 2009

Major Brian Saunders shares the following information: **Major Leticia Saunders** has been readmitted to Straub Hospital due to complications and for further testing. At this writing she has not been assigned to a room. We will share this information as soon as received. Please continue to uplift Major Leticia and family members in your prayers during these days of concern for her health.

Tuesday was perhaps the most stressful day of my life. After coming home from taking Holden to school, I helped Leticia get breakfast. But she was lethargic and uncommunicative. By now I had seen low blood sugar many times and assumed this was just another episode. After giving her glucose tablets, I waited for recovery. I tested her blood and found her sugar in the normal range. Yet she was still acting disoriented and confused. I called the doctor, who instructed me to get her to the hospital. In her confusion and delirium, Leticia simply refused to go. In any case, she was in no state to walk to the car, and I could not carry her. I ran outside and found our neighbor washing his car. He helped me get her to the car and shot out of the driveway.

Straub Hospital was only a few miles away from the house, but Honolulu traffic is notoriously slow. As we inched along my anxiety mounted: What was going on? Why was she not responding? As we pulled into the emergency entrance, Leticia began to convulse, shaking violently and thrashing around. The attendants came quickly and got her onto a gurney and into the emergency room.

It was 1:23 p.m., August 24, 2009. Leticia would never again leave the hospital.

BULLETIN

August 26, 2009

Please be in prayer for **Major Leticia Saunders**. She has been readmitted to the hospital and is in ICU. Please keep Leticia and her family in your thoughts and prayers.

Leticia had had a stroke. She was now in ICU, with a breathing tube inserted. She would be sedated to allow the brain to heal. The next 36 hours were intensely emotional. I was filled with anxiety: What damage had been done? Would she be incapacitated? Would her brain be OK? What about her body—would she be paralyzed? Some friends stayed at the hospital with me. Others took Holden to and from school. Then Holden would visit his mom, and I would take him home at night. We prayed and assured each other that this was just another in a long line of medical hurdles that we would jump over, and carry on.

BULLETIN
August 28, 2009

An update on **Major Leticia Saunders:**

Test results confirmed that Leticia suffered a stroke. Doctors are advising that the effects of this should be short–term. Brian's specific prayer request is that the effects of the stroke are indeed short–term and that Leticia's kidney function returns to normal.

Please continue to pray for Brian and Holden.

When they brought Leticia out of sedation, I literally held my breath. The breathing tube was removed, and we waited for her to gain consciousness. When she came around, her first words were in Spanish—her first language. The immediate hypothesis was that she had lost some mental function and had reverted to the language she had learned as a child. She was also hallucinating, talking of the monkeys behind the curtains in the room. The assumption was that she had lost a significant portion of cerebral capacity.

Needless to say, I was petrified. My worst fears were being realized. I remember feeling helpless, scared, and unsure of what to do or even how to pray. The doctors offered hope. They said, "This is normal at first ... give it time ... she may still retain a percentage of herself." The words sounded hollow. There was no evidence of any recovery. I thought, *No doubt they are just saying that to ease my panic. Just part of their bedside manner.* But they were correct. Within hours, Leticia was seeing, thinking, and talking more clearly—and in English. Most important of all, when I brought Holden to see her that night, she recognized him.

After a week in the ICU, Leticia was moved to a regular room. While her mental capacity appeared to show promise, she had a long way to go. The plan was to deal with the effects of the stroke first, then get back to the intestinal issue. We put family pictures up on the walls and hung them from the IV stands. I showed Leticia the pictures and reminded her of names and places. Slowly but surely, within days, her memory began to come back. We watched TV so she could see familiar sights. I read children's books, newspapers, and magazines to her. Soon, she started reading them herself.

Physical therapy was a bit more challenging, not so much because of the stroke but because her legs had begun to atrophy. The rapid fluctuations in weight over the previous several months had also left her unbalanced and unsteady on her feet. This was all extremely frustrating for Leticia—she was used to getting along on her own, handling things, and getting the job done. Suddenly she could not control her own body; she was restricted to bed and could only be mobile with the help of others. More hurdles.

BULLETIN
September 1, 2009

An update on **Major Leticia Saunders**: Praise God, Leticia has shown some marked improvement. Please continue to keep Leticia and her family in your prayers as she continues to recover. Leticia is very grateful for all the wonderful prayer support.

BULLETIN
September 2, 2009

An update and prayer request for **Major Leticia Saunders**: Leticia's kidney function has worsened, due to the stroke, the wear and tear of the past couple of weeks, rejection, and a virus which has spread from the lungs to the heart. She was given transfusions of both blood and platelets today. Tomorrow at 7 a.m. they will do a biopsy on the kidney to more accurately determine its health and the cause of the decrease in function. Pray that the biopsy is without complication, that it gives clear results, and, most important, that the kidney function returns to normal levels. Good news on cognitive function: memory is improving every day.

Each time the doctors thought they had things under control, another setback would occur. Every week we prepared for her to come home, only to find that something else had gone wrong and she would need to stay a while longer. Each time they thought she was improving, she contracted another infection. They set up her room as a mini–isolation room; visitors had to wear gloves and masks, and the equipment used was designated for her alone. All the while doctors continued to search for ways to solve the long–term problem of getting adequate nutrition into her body.

BULLETIN
September 18, 2009

An update from Major Brian Saunders regarding Leticia:

It appears we have hit a bit of a speed–bump on Leticia's road to recovery. She has been readmitted to ICU due to complications. She was having trouble breathing last night and was placed back on a breathing machine. It appears she has a new infection in her lungs. They are investigating its cause and testing to see if it is in her bloodstream. She is awake and doing fine—hungry since they won't let her eat—but will remain in ICU until they determine what happened. It will also set back the physical therapy a bit, but that cannot be helped. Your prayers are very much appreciated!

Blessings, Brian

Summer turned into fall. Our family settled into what became our new pattern for daily life. I would take Holden to school in the morning, then visit Leticia in the hospital for a couple of hours before heading to the office. In the afternoon, I would pick Holden up, and we would spend the afternoon and evening at the hospital with Leticia. Holden would do his homework in the corner, and Leticia and I would work on whatever projects needed to get done for the corps (church). I eventually obtained a notebook computer to make it easier to get work done at the hospital. Our corps had evening activities several nights a week, so I would often leave to lead programs, then come back in time to say good night and take Holden home.

BULLETIN
September 30, 2009

From Major Brian Saunders: "Here's the latest on Leticia: Unfortunately, the pneumonia appears to have come back into her lungs. She had a difficult time breathing the night before last, due to the lungs filling up, and they had to put the oxygen mask back on. The lungs are still clouded today, but she is breathing better. So, another round of antibiotics. The good news is that the dialysis is working well to decrease the excess fluid, which should help enable her to begin exercising her legs. Her kidney function has not improved and she may need to stay on dialysis after she is released from the hospital—not sure if that will be temporary at this point. Still no word on when she may be released. She's in great spirits and is witnessing to the staff at the hospital. Thanks again for your prayers."

Holden and I ate dinner almost every night in the hospital cafeteria or in Leticia's room. We got to know the doctors, nurses, and other staff. The hospital staff became extended members of our family. The cafeteria crew called us by name and even knew our dinner orders before we placed them. Tuesday was "open–faced turkey sandwich night"—a favorite of ours. As the weeks stretched into months, this surreal routine became quite normal. But we kept assuming Leticia would soon come home. We had a ramp built across the front steps and set up an office for her at the house. Ever the optimist, I never considered the alternative.

We discovered that we had a ministry there on the fourth floor. Leticia was quite open with her faith, and the nurses often found her reading her Bible. She shared verses with them; much later, several nurses told me how her testimony had been instrumental in their own lives. She arranged for candy to be delivered to the nurses on Halloween and wrote notes of thanks and encouragement to the doctors. Straub is a teaching hospital, and I would sometimes arrive at her room to find student nurses seated in a semicircle around her bed as she told them about diabetes, how it feels to get IVs, or how best to soothe a patient in distress—all from the perspective of the patient.

BULLETIN
October 9, 2009

An update from Major Brian Saunders: "Leticia is still in the hospital, under antiviral meds to knock down the pneumonia and other infections and awaiting determination on the long–term health of her kidney. (Side note: This week marked the seventh anniversary of the transplant!) She appreciates everyone's prayers."

Leticia continued working from bed. She dealt with paperwork, did the corps statistics, filled out the cards to put on the Army's Christmas "Angel Tree" displays, and even wrote the kids' Christmas play. Still, every medical advance was followed by a setback. Each time the doctors thought they were making progress, a new challenge would arise.

From: Brian Saunders
To: Hawaiian & Pacific Islands Officers
Date: October 13, 2009, 9:34 AM

Dear Colleagues,

As I write this, most of you are gathering on Kauai [the northernmost of the Hawaiian Islands] for Officers Councils [a meeting of officers in the Hawaiian and Pacific Islands Division]. Regretfully, Leticia and I will not be able to join you this year. I do, however, want to share with you Leticia's prayer from this morning. She prayed specifically that God would refresh your hearts, your minds, and your souls; that you would grow closer to God, to His mission, and to each other through your time together; and that God would richly bless you during these days. Her prayer each day is that God would be glorified through her illness, and that He would use it to somehow draw others closer to Him. I assure you He already has. Councils is an important time of spiritual and physical refreshment, and we know that God will bless you as you gather to fellowship and soak in His Word and His will.

Thank you to each of you for your continued support and prayer. Leticia continues to recover, albeit very slowly. ... She is in "serious but stable" condition but grows a bit stronger day by day. ... Pray too for Holden—he's a trouper and is handling this all as well as anyone could. Still, it's not easy to see Mom in the hospital day after day, and your prayers on his behalf are appreciated and felt.

Leticia asked me specifically to let you know that she is praying for each of you by name today—that God would enrich and fill you; that you would find something new in God, in your ministry, in your relationships that brings you closer to Him and to those you serve. God be with you.

Blessings to you all,

Brian

BULLETIN

November 4, 2009

An update on Major Leticia Saunders from Brian: Leticia continues to reign as the "pink princess" of the fourth floor. In her pink sweat jacket and hair band, under her pink and green blanket, she continues to defy the odds as she battles the various infections and viruses that are attacking her body. Her leg muscles have atrophied, but physical therapy and her own personally designed exercises are helping to increase strength and muscle mass. Between dialysis, doctors' visits and tests, she is busy filling out Angel Tree cards and writing the corps Christmas programs. Oh, and once in a while, they let her rest.

The Christmas season is a very busy time for The Salvation Army. Fund–raising, social services, and special programs all compete for time and attention. With Leticia in the hospital, and me balancing hospital time, dad duties, and work, I realized we would need help. I asked my parents to come and stay with us to help with the Army's red kettle fund–raising program and brought in two cadets (Salvation Army officers–in–training) to assist with the corps programs. Even so, I felt myself tugged in all directions. I wanted to continue to do it all—to be there for Leticia, to care for Holden, and to still run the corps and all its programs. For the most part, I was successful—perhaps because I continued to assume that

Leticia would get better; perhaps because I was too busy to think about it; or maybe because I subconsciously used the busyness to block any negative thoughts.

By outward appearances, everything seemed to be working out: Leticia was stable—albeit growing increasingly frustrated with her lack of mobility—and the corps programs were all continuing as normal. The busiest month of the year was unfolding and I seemed to have everything in hand. Until Thanksgiving.

A few days before the holiday, Leticia's condition suddenly took a turn for the worse. Her kidney function decreased dramatically, and she had to be placed on around–the–clock dialysis once again. An infection had spread to her bloodstream and was now affecting several vital organs. Her body was shutting down. She was unconscious and the doctor was concerned that she might never recover.

From across her bed in the ICU, the doctor gave me the "Be prepared" speech. I simply could not—would not—believe it. After all we'd been through, after all Leticia had survived, surely she'd pull out of this as well—she always had before! In fact, the doctors had given us grave diagnoses so many times before, Holden and I tended to shrug them off. "Dr. Doom came to see me again," I'd say.

"The usual?" Holden would respond.

"Yeah, but you know Mom, she'll prove them wrong again." And by Thanksgiving Day, it seemed she had. She was awake and alert when I arrived. We talked and joked and laughed off the latest predictions of doom. I even felt confident enough to leave her to participate in the Salvation Army's Community Thanksgiving Luncheon at the convention center across the street. A holiday miracle, I told people—Leticia recovered just in time to celebrate the day. Later, Holden brought a full gluten–free Thanksgiving meal for her and we shared a little family holiday together there in the ICU. It would be our last.

From: **Brian Saunders**
To: **Undisclosed recipients**
Date: **November 28, 2009, 10:37 PM**

Dear family & friends,

There is both good news and bad news to report this week. First the bad news: Leticia has contracted yet another virus—this one a particularly dangerous fungus in the bloodstream. The good news is that she has been released from ICU and is now back in a regular "monitored" room. They took her off the 24/7 dialysis machine last night, and she has remained stable enough to graduate back to the regular dialysis regimen. For most of the last two weeks, while she has been in ICU, she has remained asleep or extremely drowsy, due both to the level of pain medication and the fact that her body was using all its energy reserves to battle the virus. Her body was gradually being drained of its resources. But get this! On Thanksgiving, she woke up refreshed, revived and pain–free. She ate not only her hospital breakfast but also the Thanksgiving dinner that Holden and my mom had prepared for her. She has been awake virtually the entire day. I believe we have seen a miracle. She is not out of the woods yet, but she is on the path.

Leticia and I have come up with a phrase: *Just one more*. It answers the question we have heard all too often of late: "How much more can her body take?" It's the answer to the questions, "What more does God want of us; what more can God expect her to deal with?" God calls on us to have faith—to trust Him. Not for the distant future, but for today; for the current crisis. We need not worry about what's going to happen tomorrow; just trust Him for today. The Israelites in the wilderness gathered manna one day at a time, demonstrating their faith for each day, trusting that God would come through again the next day. Today, God is asking our family to trust Him through one more illness, one more medical crisis. *One at a time*. So, we trust Him: one illness, one crisis at a time. We need not worry about the future, just trust Him for today. So, how much more? *Just one more*. How much more can Leticia take? *Just one more. One at a time*. And when that crisis is behind us, we are ready to trust Him for the next one, and, if necessary, the next one. Always, it is *just one more*.

So, we thank you all for your prayers and thoughts, and ask that you continue to pray—and have faith—that God will demonstrate His power, and that Leticia will continue to have victory over just one more, each and every time.

Blessings,

Brian

As Leticia recovered, she was moved back to a regular room. The doctors allowed visitors again, and evenings were spent with friends and family. We played cards and table games, opened Christmas cards, and shared stories. Still, the infections remained and she continued 24–hour dialysis while doctors monitored her kidney decline. Within two weeks, she had slipped again, becoming very weak, spending much of the day asleep. Visits ceased again in order to guard against infection; physical therapy ground to a halt because she was too weak to participate.

From: **Brian Saunders**
To: **Undisclosed recipients**
Date: **December 6, 2009, 11:26 PM**
Re: **Leticia's Progress**

Dear family & friends,

A bit of bad news to report this week. This afternoon, Leticia was admitted to ICU again, this time due to complications arising from low blood pressure. At this early stage, they believe the low blood pressure is being caused by yet another infection. They are running blood tests to confirm. In the meantime, they pulled the IV central line to test it, and, despite having troubles before, managed to insert a new central one. They have re–commenced 24/7 dialysis and given her another blood transfusion. So, another "just one more" hurdle.
Thanks for your continued support and prayers.

Blessings,

Brian

As the second week of December arrived, Leticia continued to hover between critical and stable. When she was awake, she was cheerful and upbeat, but she spent much of the day sleeping. She needed the oxygen mask more and more frequently. The doctors began making those "Be prepared" comments again.

On Friday, December 11, I spent the evening at the hospital. Holden was at home. Leticia was in deep sleep, with the dialysis machine and breathing mask in continual use. She had been like that for almost two days. Around 10 p.m., I tucked her in and headed for home. An hour later I got a call from the hospital. "Come to the hospital. Your wife wants to see you." I left the house without waking either my parents or Holden and sped there. *Wow, she's awake! Maybe we are finally making some progress. Perhaps sleeping for so long helped to strengthen her body and purge the infection.*

When I arrived, Leticia was awake and alert. The breathing mask was off to one side of the pillow. She took my hand, took a breath, and said simply, "I met with God tonight. It's time for me to go Home." I understood. And I knew she was serious. I also knew that she would have kept fighting forever if God had not told her otherwise. She was a true survivor; always rising to whatever challenge was before her—be it building a community center, doing the church statistics, or fighting for her own health. She loved Holden and me too much to simply give up. Nothing on Earth would have stopped her from fighting to get better—but that's just it:

This wasn't something on Earth—it was from Heaven; it was from God Himself. He had told her it was time to come Home.

We talked about a number of things that night. Our ministry, our marriage, our family. Leticia reminded me that Holden would now be solely my responsibility. She charged me with protecting his heart and guiding his soul. We talked about his emotions and his spiritual life and how her death would forever change him. Her only concern about dying was how it would affect Holden. She was determined that I do my best to ensure that her death would not embitter him against God. Around 6 a.m., she told me to go home and get Holden.

BULLETIN
December 12, 2009

This evening Major Leticia Saunders' health condition took a turn for the worse and while Leticia is at peace with God's will, the Saunders covet your prayers for Leticia, Brian, Holden, and the family.

When we returned to the hospital, Leticia was still awake, waiting for us. She knew this would be our last conversation. The next half-hour was special indeed. In those moments, room 427 became sacred space, holy ground. Much of what we talked about will remain just between us, but I can share a couple of things. Leticia reminded us that we would now be a team of two, and that we would need to be there for each other, supporting each other as we learned to live without her. She told Holden, "Take care of Dad," and reminded me again that it was now my sole responsibility to deliver Holden safely into manhood. To guard his soul. A sacred task. Mostly, she asked us simply to honor God's will, to let her go Home. Within minutes, she faded. Her eyes closed, and her head turned to the side, resting on the pillow. She was smiling. It was as if she had held on long enough to give us this final blessing, and then dismissed Earth, and turned her heart to God. She was done here, and was now looking toward Heaven.

From: **Edward Hill**
To: **Hawaiian & Pacific Islands Division Officers**
Date: **December 12, 2009, 4:03 PM**

I am sad to share with you that Major Leticia Saunders has been moved to what is described as "comfort care" at Straub Hospital. Within days, it is expected that she will go to be with the Lord. I know this comes as tragic news, but be assured of Leticia's strong faith during these past days. She believes that the Lord is calling her to be with Him forever. Even in these hours, she radiates the joy of the Lord.

Brian and Holden are grieving but also full of faith in God's goodness and faithfulness.

I will keep all of you informed of what transpires in the coming days. I would simply ask you to pray now that God's will be done and that He bring peace to Brian and Holden and all family and friends.

God bless you all.

Edward Hill, Major
Divisional Commander
Hawaiian and Pacific Islands

The doctors came in and told us that there was now no chance of recovery. I said I already knew that. That she had told me. A few curious glances, but they knew Leticia had been awake. I numbly signed the papers. They disconnected the machines and moved her to a "comfort room." At that point, the doctors said she had 24 to 72 hours. She never regained consciousness.

Holden and I decided together that we would stay with her—just us, our little family—waiting on God. Holden asked for a monitor to be placed in the room so we could watch her progress. He actually ran the blood pressure machine when her pressure got too low to be recorded automatically. She remained stable all through Saturday and Sunday and into Monday afternoon. She was given sedatives and pain relievers intravenously to keep her comfortable.

Holden suggested that we thank all his mom's doctors and nurses, so we made quick rounds in the hospital, thanking them for their work and inviting them to her funeral. After all, we had seen them every day for the past four months—they were now part of our family. Over the weekend, and especially on Monday, many hospital staff members came to see us in Leticia's room. They shared with us how she had blessed them or encouraged them or taught them.

At one point, I arrived in the room to find three nurses flipping through Leticia's Bible, which I had left open on her bed. My first reaction was annoyance. How dare they come in here and just pick up something that was not theirs! Something so personal and sacred! But then they showed me that they were looking for a verse that Leticia had shared with them, one that had encouraged them as they worked toward their nursing degrees. A long conversation on faith and eternity followed. I am humbled by the knowledge that Leticia continued her ministry through those four months in the hospital, and that her lasting legacy is not limited to those she touched during her active service as an officer, but extends even to her final caregivers.

BULLETIN
December 14, 2009

It is fully expected that **Major Leticia Saunders** will be Promoted to Glory in the next day or so. Major Brian and Holden truly appreciate the prayerful support that has been given them by comrades throughout the Western Territory. While they are grieving, they are also fully confident in God's goodness and faithfulness. Leticia has expressed that she is ready to be with the Lord forever. We celebrate the imminent reality of her future glory.

God bless you.
Edward Hill, Major
Divisional Commander Hawaiian and Pacific Islands

Finally, at about 3 p.m., Leticia's heart and breathing rates began to decline. Nothing can prepare you for this. Holden kept a hand on the blood pressure monitor. Soon, it became too low to register. Nothing. The room monitors were turned off, so there was no "flatline" tone signifying her death. Just silence. After what seemed an eternity, I leaned forward and kissed her forehead. Holden and I held her hands as God ushered her Home. A sacred moment, a holy moment. Our final minutes as a family—at least for this life.

For years Leticia had joked that as soon as she reached Heaven, she would scarf down a plate of baklava—a big no—

no for someone with both diabetes and celiac disease. Holden commented a few minutes later that she was probably already on her third plate. That was a good moment for me. Simple words, but rich in meaning. I understood in that instant that Holden knew—and trusted beyond a shadow of a doubt—that Mom was in Heaven. I knew he was going to be OK. I kissed her forehead one more time. With a last glance back, Holden and I left the room.

Early that morning I had prepared an outgoing message on my phone, set up to send to my entire contact list. At 3:40 that afternoon, December 14, 2009, I pressed "Send." The message read simply, "Leticia has gone Home."

BULLETIN
December 14, 2009

Major Leticia Saunders was Promoted to Glory this afternoon, December 14, 2009, in Honolulu, Hawaii. Major Brian Saunders, with assistance from his father & mother and divisional staff in Hawaii, will prepare a proper Promoted to Glory bulletin honoring Leticia and providing details for her funeral and memorial service.

Majors Neil & Beth Saunders have been with Brian, Leticia and Holden, assisting with Christmas activities at the corps and helping out with various family needs during this difficult time of Leticia's hospitalization. We rejoice with the Saunders family as they express a continuing sense of peace with God's will for Leticia's life, which was filled with love and fulfilled ministry.

Please continue to pray for Brian and Holden for strength and peace and wonderful memories of Leticia as wife, soulmate, and mother.

From: **Brian Saunders**
To: **Undisclosed recipients**
Date: **December 16, 2009, 1:14 AM**

My Dear Friends,

By now most of you are aware that Leticia was "promoted to Glory" the day before yesterday. With your permission, I'll share just one more update ...

I shared with you last month about our *just one more* philosophy—that God had been asking us to trust Him one day, one illness, one hurdle at a time.

It turns out that the last hurdle was not meant for Leticia at all, but for me. God was now asking me to trust Him with Leticia just one last time. This time, the hurdle was not her health, but her life: to let her go, to let her go Home. The hardest task of all. It is done.

I thank God for Leticia—my partner in both life and ministry. He shared her with me for 20 years, and for that I will be forever grateful. She is the smartest, most beautiful, most creative person I know. I miss her.

Many of you were present at Territorial Officers Councils in Los Angeles in June. Leticia gave her testimony, sharing that "It's OK not to be OK." Despite our shortcomings, failings and problems—be it health or otherwise—God still loves us, and God will get us through. God can still use us. God does not need us to be perfect, just ready. It's OK not to be OK. Turns out that was the last time she spoke in public. Right now, Holden and I are decidedly not OK—and I am OK with that. I'm OK with not being OK because I know that God is with us, and that we will—someday—be OK. With God's support, we will start our new life together—without his mom, without my partner, but still with God. I'm not sure what happens next. I have no idea how to go on, how to face this. I don't know why God allowed this to happen, but I know she's Home—where she always wanted to be. The Bible reminds us that as Christians, our citizenship is in Heaven. So she is where she belongs. I must confess these words sound hollow right now—clichés that I'll cling to in the hope that they are true.

Thank you each for your prayers and support. It is more meaningful than I have words to express. Thank you for upholding us. We feel your prayers as we feel God's hands beneath us.

Brian

I believe God was kind in the timing of Leticia's illness and death. Throughout those four months of hospitalization, I, along with just about everyone else, remained optimistic. I just took it for granted that Leticia would recover—as she had always done before. I trusted God and knew that He would work things out for the best. Perhaps this was avoidance or just plain naiveté, but I think of it as faith. For most of those four months, there really was no reason to doubt that Leticia would recover. I trusted all would be well. Once Leticia told me of her conversation with God, however, I was able to accept that she would not be getting better.

I had two days to get used to the idea of the reality of her death. I think the timing was about right: Had I known for an extended period of time that she was going to die, or had she lingered for more than those two days, I am sure I would have built up much more anxiety and sunk deeper into depression. If she had died instantly after the stroke, I would have been in total shock and not known which way to turn. As it was, the timing was beneficial—just enough time to get used to it without having to go through a prolonged period of pre–death grief.

It was that last talk with Leticia that—in some small yet important measure—prepared me. I believe it was a true gift from God—an opportunity to say goodbye, to bless and be blessed, and to pronounce a benediction on our earthly lives together. She prepared me for her own death. She understood that she had completed all that God wanted from her here on earth, and it was OK for her to come Home now. Even as she faded, she seem concerned that I understand that it was not so much that she wanted to go—no, she loved Holden and me, and was so sorry that she was going to miss seeing him growing up—but that she had to obey God, to stop resisting and simply go. She pronounced a blessing upon me as her last words on Earth.

That conversation gave me strength and conviction that I would not have believed possible. It gave me the assurance of her love, a purpose for my life without her, and the will to fulfill her legacy. Those few minutes have carried me as I journey through this valley.

Leticia Adams Saunders

January 2, 1962–December 14, 2009

Leticia Saunders, faithful Christian, mother, wife and minister, was promoted to Glory on Monday, December 14, from Honolulu, Hawaii.

Leticia Adams was born to Alan and Lucrecia Adams on January 2, 1962, in National City, California. Mom, Dad, and Lettie soon welcomed a little brother, Alex, and the family was complete. Leticia enjoyed a happy, loving childhood, filled with memories of vacations in Mexico, afternoons at the beach, and Saturdays spent motorcycling in the desert. In high school, she was in the National Honor Society and a varsity cheerleader— she graduated a year early.

When Leticia was 13, she was introduced to The Salvation Army through the Girl Guard program. She soon began attending this new church, becoming accustomed to its unique traditions and language. (Apparently not quite quickly enough: she liked to tell the story of her first Sunday at San Diego Citadel. When it was announced that someone had been "Promoted to Glory," she burst into applause—only to stop immediately as people turned to glare at her with a mix of amusement and incredulity.)

After working as youth minister and accountant at the Santa Rosa, Medford, and LaGrande corps, Leticia entered training school in 1989 as a member of the "Servants of Jesus" session. She met Brian there, and their romance and love blossomed as they studied the art and craft of ministry. Upon commissioning and ordination, Leticia was appointed as assistant at the Pasadena Tabernacle Corps, while Brian was assigned to the Training School. They were married at the Pasadena Tabernacle on December 27, 1991, after which Leticia took up her new appointment with Brian at the School for Officer Training. Their ministry took them around the world, with appointments at the School for Officer Training in California, the Portland Tabernacle Corps in Oregon, the Dunstable Corps in England, the School for Continuing Education in California, the Salem Citadel Corps in Oregon, Guam, and finally, the Kauluwela Mission Corps in Honolulu.

Leticia was a creative artist, a gifted preacher, and an insightful teacher. She relished the ministry of sharing the depth of God's Word and will with others, while at the same time she enjoyed the creative opportunities of programming—she even loved napkin folding at Crestmont! Even so, family was always first. Leticia ensured that Holden and Brian were always her priority—both in ministry and in life. Our most important congregation, Leticia would often say, is our son.

Leticia often described herself as a survivor. She joked that she collected diseases like other people collected trinkets. Still, she never let her physical limitations get in the way of her life. She ministered, traveled, laughed, and loved. During these last four months in the hospital, her cheerful and faithful spirit strengthened staff members and family alike. God gave her the strength to survive and thrive—until the day He asked her to come Home.

Leticia will be missed as an officer, a friend, a family member, a wife, and a mom. She is survived by her husband, Brian, her son, Holden, her father, Alan Adams, her brother, Alex Adams and his wife, Yvette, with their children, Joshua and Christina, her aunt, Margaret Ross, as well as other family members. Her delight was in the Lord, and on December 14, He gave her the desire of her heart. (Psalm 37:4)

Into the valley

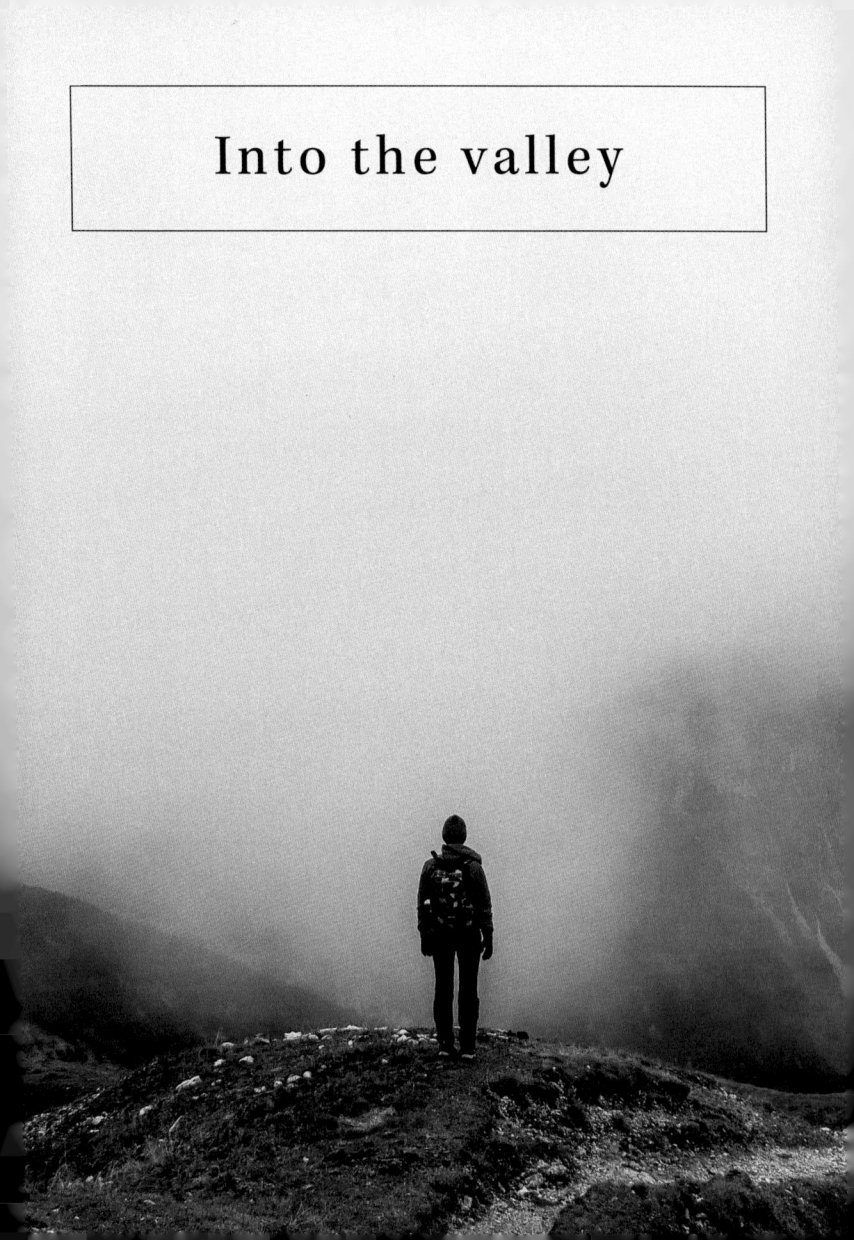

"

I knew that I was in shock and
that I was not truly processing
Leticia's death. I knew I was
going to have to go through
the stages of grief.

"

THREE

I COULDN'T SEE THE VALLEY AT FIRST. The path ahead of us was obscured. It was all I could do to put one foot in front of the other. To get out of bed. To breathe. Contemplating anything further out than today seemed too heavy a task.

These were dark days. The pain was so real, so visceral. It was hard to imagine carrying on without Leticia; it was so difficult to watch the world around me move while I stood still. I wanted to cry out to everyone, "Hey, stop! Can't you see that everything is different now? Why are you carrying on like nothing happened?" World affairs and local events lost their importance. The Earth continued to revolve. People went to work; life carried on as usual—for everyone but me. For me, everything came to a screeching halt.

In quiet moments I caught a glimpse of the path before us—the long, difficult journey upon which Holden and I were setting out. But I kept that image at bay by staying busy with the present: the steps right in front of me were all I wanted to deal with. I could handle today—it was tomorrow I could not bear thinking about. Holden and I were undoubtedly experiencing the "normal" emotions of the moment: shock, disbelief, and a numbness that permeated heart and soul.

I was on automatic pilot—going through the motions, dealing with things, making arrangements, all with little thought about the long–term. I had tasks to perform, duties that required my attention. I had a funeral to plan. Fortunately, I did not have to do it alone.

Arms extended …

It was very good to have my parents staying with us. For the past three Christmas seasons, they had come to Honolulu to assist with myriad Christmas activities at the corps. Now they were just where God knew they needed to be. My folks knew when Holden and I needed space and knew to be around when we wanted company. My mom took care of all the household needs. Holden and I came and went, knowing that all was in order at home.

At the corps, the team was hard at work. Christmas kettles, toy distribution, and corps programming all continued in my absence. My parents, corps leaders, staff members, and other officers simply got busy doing the work, ensuring that I was free to spend time as I needed to.

What I did not realize at the time was how important this was to them. During those last two weeks of December, they pitched in—helping, supporting, just "being there." It was their way of dealing with their own loss. By allowing them to help, in whatever manner they could, I gave them permission to grieve alongside Holden and me—to come into our pain and, together, to find a way through it.

Like just about any leaders, Salvation Army officers can be tempted to view ourselves as being indispensible—to feel that the ministry will fall apart if we are not there. This is certainly something I was guilty of in the early months of Leticia's illness. I thought I could do it all: be at the hospital with Leticia, take care of Holden, and run the business and ministry of the Army at the same time. It's probably something I have been guilty of for a long time. I wanted to be the perfect husband, father, and minister, all at once. Leticia knew better; she knew how to pace herself, to say "no" when needed and to strike the right balance between ministry and family. It took me much longer to figure this out.

While as early as mid–November I realized that I would need additional staff to cover for Leticia and me during the busy Christmas season, I still felt I needed to be on top of everything myself. In the final weeks of the season, I managed to come to work less, allowing myself to spend more time with Leticia. I discovered that despite the fact that this was the busiest time of the year—critical, time–consuming fund–raising; massive toy drives and gift distributions; countless public relations events on top of the busy church schedule—the ministry seemed to move right on along without me. In the week following Leticia's passing, I relinquished all responsibilities and focused on Holden and the funeral arrangements. The team simply took over.

Time to catch our breath

Being freed from ministry responsibilities enabled me not only to work on funeral arrangements but also to spend time with Holden. We were given the gift of time and space—to plan the ceremony, to share memories, and just to be together. In fact, just as Holden wanted to stay with Mom during those last three days of her life, he now insisted on staying with me.

We did everything together, from choosing the songs and participants for two services—one in Hawaii and one in California—to meeting with the funeral director to picking up the death certificate. Holden sustained me as much as I sustained him. As Leticia had told us, we were now a team of two, and we would need to support each other. So we did just that. We went to the beach to watch the waves, cooked meals, and visited with friends, all as we prepared Leticia's funeral. During those initial days of intense sorrow, we needed time and space. Time to breathe; time to get accustomed to a new reality; time to reflect, to remember, and to re-focus on what mattered now.

Walking alongside

It is a shame that so few men can claim real friendships. I count myself blessed to be one of the few. Since childhood,

Craig Bowler and Ivan Wild have been my closest friends. Over the years, we moved, married, started careers (all in the ministry), and had children. We were each other's groomsmen, godfathers to each other's children, confidants, accountability partners, and friends. We know each other's secrets, gifts, and faults. We call and correspond on a weekly basis. We share each other's burdens and joys. We offer encouragement, advice, and counsel to one another. We call each other out when necessary. No matter where we live in the world, or how busy we are, we get together once a year for a weekend of "peer mentorship."

During the long months of Leticia's hospitalization, I shared all the ups and downs with Craig and Ivan. We talked on the phone frequently; I could call them at any time of day or night with news—good or bad. They were always interested and always concerned, and they always prayed with me. Immediately upon hearing of Leticia's death, they flew to Honolulu—Craig from Atlanta, and Ivan from Los Angeles.

With these two, I could feel free to express my emotions without fear of judgment or pity. They helped organize the funerals, handled details, and made a point of getting Holden and me out of the house. We played tourist, went to the beach, took long drives. Time well spent.

In the months after Leticia's death, Ivan and Craig continued to be there for me. They called and/or wrote just about every day, always with a word of encouragement and genuine care. Sometimes they said nothing at all.

Holden and I were also fortunate to have an extensive network of friends and family. Calls, cards, and emails came in from around the world. The condolences and clichés became real: "She's better off," "No more pain," "She's in the presence of God," became more than mere words of comfort: they were the truth being spoken into my wounded soul. Truth that, despite the corny words, I needed to hear.

Pastors to the pastor

I am more convinced than ever that there is no more significant role for the officer or pastor than ministry in times of illness and grief. During the months of Leticia's illness, the officers of the Hawaiian and Pacific Islands Division surrounded us with prayer and presence. When Leticia was in the ICU after the stroke, many officers visited and called.

Here's something I will never forget: On the day of Leticia's death, Major (now Lt. Colonel) Edward "Dusty" Hill, then the commander of the Hawaii and Pacific Islands Division, texted me early in the morning to say he was in the hospital dining room. He said he just wanted to be around and to call him if and when we wanted to. He waited there all day. Now, I am sure that, as the divisional commander, he had myriad responsibilities to attend to. It was, after all, a Monday, two weeks before Christmas. Yet he sat there, hour after hour, holding his own private vigil as Holden and I sat with Leticia three floors above him. Finally, just before 4 p.m., I called him to let him know Leticia was gone. He was with us five minutes later. Dusty demonstrated true pastoral care. Silent. Available. Present. Constant. I will forever be grateful.

Further afield, (Colonel) Dave Hudson continued to provide support and blessing after Leticia died. He called every day at first, then every week and, eventually, once a month. (To this day, both Dusty and Dave continue to check in with me regularly.) This was pastoral care at its most intimate and most immediate. Craig, Ivan, Dusty, and Dave were there when needed but did not crowd or patronize. None offered easy, pat answers. They continued to show interest long after the rest of the world had gotten back to "normal." They understood that grief is a long–term ailment, that it does not go away when you go back to work. The ministry of these four men, along with many others, had an immeasurable impact on my life when I was most vulnerable.

'Physician, heal thyself'

As an officer, over the years I had assisted many families with funeral arrangements, guiding them and pastoring them through their grief. Now, I had this odd sense of being able to counsel and guide myself. I knew what should be said and done; I knew what advice and condolences people would give to me, and I knew how to say those things to myself. It's an interesting thing to watch oneself going through the grieving process. It was almost surreal—a kind of out–of–body experience.

I knew that I was in shock and that I was not truly processing Leticia's death. I knew I was going to have to go through the stages of grief. I understood that I did not fully appreciate the weight of the loss yet. I knew that it would soon hit and that I would need to express my grief before it consumed me. I also knew the process of the business of death: contacting the funeral home, making arrangements, obtaining death certificates, changing names on bank accounts, notifying Social Security, etc. I wrote out a long to-do list and simply went through it.

I'm the kind of person who needs to be busy, and one of my most obvious coping mechanisms was to get back to work—at least partially. Even before the Honolulu funeral, I began dealing with some ministry-related duties. Christmas Sunday was fast approaching, and the final few days of the red kettle campaign were upon us. For me, it was good to regain some sense of regularity and normalcy. I knew keeping busy to be a classic coping mechanism. It borders on avoidance, but I purposefully forced myself not to do too much—as much in appreciation for those who were working so hard on my behalf as for myself.

'Hiding' on Christmas Sunday

Leticia went Home on December 14, 2009. The first of her two funerals was planned for December 20—Christmas Sunday. Everything had already been planned for the Christmas service at the corps: the kids' play, the special music, the visit from Santa loaded with gifts for the children. The church had forgone the regular worship service the previous Sunday, instead holding a prayer service as Holden and I held our little family vigil in Leticia's hospital room.

So I insisted that the worship service this Sunday go forward as planned. The kids had worked hard on the play; it was Christmas, and the church deserved to celebrate the day. I even led the service that day—although it was arranged to have someone else preach. The funeral was set for the afternoon. The poignancy was not lost on anyone: On the very day of Letitia's funeral, the kids performed the play that she had written from her hospital bed. The props were moved away just in time for her casket to be rolled in.

In retrospect, I can see that several emotions and convictions were competing that day. First, I was still in a state of shock. I was acting on instinct—going through the motions, running on adrenaline, doing what was necessary. It was Sunday; I was the corps officer. I was fulfilling my duties, making sure things carried on as usual and not recognizing the fact that this day was anything but usual. I thought that the congregation should not suffer just because I was hurting. I didn't want them to feel the pain that I was feeling. I didn't understand that they were also in pain. They knew the day was not the same; they would have been OK with whatever transpired. I wanted everything to be normal for the congregation, and didn't understand that no one expected it to be so.

But there was more to it than that. I didn't want people to

see my pain or to think that I couldn't "handle it." This was purely subconscious—I certainly was not aware of trying to hide my feelings. I wanted to be able to still do everything and to project this image of strength and control. All day long, people kept saying, "You're doing so well." What exactly does that mean?! Only now do I begin to understand that "doing well" is a façade, a fallacy that we somehow associate with the appearance of a lack of emotion. For some reason, we have this compulsion to appear "strong." We even label tears as "breaking down," as if it is something to be avoided, evidence of damage that needs to be repaired.

In his book, *Pastor as a Person,* Gary Harbaugh reminds us that the pastor is a whole person—physical, emotional, mental, social—all connected to the self and indivisible from the ministry. I was trying to divide myself into two people, the grieving husband and the efficient, energetic leader. I did not recognize that I could *not* separate the two—that I needed to fully embrace the overarching need to be myself, and not worry about what others might think. I needed to be my "whole self"—both pastor and husband.

Two funerals

I spoke at Leticia's funeral in Honolulu. I shared stories of poignancy and respect for the woman who had changed my life and given me so much. I spoke of the cliff–diving rock at Waimea Bay on the North Shore of Oahu. How it was as if Leticia was standing high on that rock as all her illnesses and diseases crashed against her from below. How God was her Rock, holding her above it all. And how God had now simply come and scooped her up, where the waves could not reach her anymore. I talked about one of her favorite hymns, *"It Is Well with My Soul,"* and that now, as never before, it was truly well with Leticia's soul. In The Salvation Army, we often refer to death as a "promotion to Glory." A bit cheesy, perhaps, but a nice sentiment. The Army paid its respects to a fallen soldier. Colonel Dave Hudson, a true friend and my mentor for many years, spoke on behalf of The Salvation Army.

Christmas Day was understandably subdued, but we tried our best to make it real. As I would soon come to realize, even the most happy occasions would now always be tinged with melancholy. The mood continually turned poignant as gifts were opened that were meant for Leticia or that she had purchased from her hospital bed. One gift in particular was special: Years before, Leticia's mother had given her a citrine stone—the November birthstone. While still in the hospital, Leticia arranged to have it mounted and asked me to give it to my mother. It was a touching moment when my mother unwrapped this family heirloom gift from her now–deceased daughter–in–law.

The next day we headed for the mainland for the second funeral, this one in Pasadena, California. The Salvation Army corps there, which I had attended during my college years and where Leticia had been the assistant corps officer prior to our marriage, was a natural location for us because it was so rich in personal history and memories. It is—if an officer can have one—our "home" corps.

Leticia's body had been cremated in Honolulu, so I carried her ashes with me on the plane. I'm not sure why, but I decided that I would physically hold them the entire trip, and I would not allow anyone else to touch the urn. Perhaps I felt just a final physical attachment. At some point it occurred to me that part of my physical body—my kidney—was in the urn as well. I was reminded of that cliché about feeling as if part of us has died when a loved one passes away. In this case, it was true in a literal sense—a part of my body had actually died with Leticia and was now mixed with her ashes in that urn.

The service at Pasadena went smoothly. Leticia's family was there and participated well. I spoke again, this time sharing our final conversation. Dave Hudson, who had been the main speaker at the funeral in Honolulu, also spoke this time.

He began, "The text message I received from Brian came as no surprise; it simply said, 'Leticia has gone home.' It made more sense to me than some of the most profound documents I have ever read. The text was not informing me that Leticia had passed away. It was letting me know that her life's ambition has now been achieved, that she is Home."

Dave spoke of Leticia's determination to be a faithful follower of the One who had called her, regardless of the cost. He suggested that it was because of God's call that this was her favorite Scripture:

Delight yourself in the Lord and he will give you the desires of your heart. Commit your way to the Lord; trust in him and he will do this: He will make your righteousness shine like the dawn, the justice of your cause like the noonday sun. Be still before the Lord and wait patiently for him; do not fret ...

(Psalm 37:4–7 NIV 1984)

Dave reminded us of Leticia's testimony at Officers Councils, when she taught that "It's OK not to be OK." He said that Leticia understood the words of Jesus in John 16:33:

I have told you these things, so that in me you may have peace. In this world you will have trouble. But take heart! I have overcome the world.

Ultimately, Dave said, what sustained Leticia in the face of overwhelmingly difficult challenges was an awareness that her life was not restricted to the confines of her time on Earth. He went on: "Someday, God's Kingdom will come in its fullness. And, while the path to His coming Kingdom may not be as direct as we would like, and our present situation may sometimes be difficult, our Christian hope is ultimately about long–term outcomes, not short–term optimism. We look forward to the day when God will make all things new. For Leticia, that day has come."

Setting off on the trail

The day after the funeral, we flew to Northern California for the committal service at a cemetery in San Francisco. We said our final farewells, Holden and I remaining at the gravesite alone until everyone else was in the cars. Alone. Yet not alone. I remember looking at the upended earth, at Holden, at the sky. I heard birds chirping, the wind whistling through the trees. And I knew, I knew, that God was there, and that when we turned and walked away, He would be with us.

Both my brother, David, and his family and my parents lived in Sacramento, so we drove there to spend New Year's together. David and Jennifer have three young children, so Holden was able to unwind with them and set aside "real life" for a while. David and I spent time talking, cooking, and organizing activities with the kids. Mostly, it was time away from the realities of Honolulu. In a way, it was pure avoidance.

One of those "rules of grief" that, as a minister, I know all too well, is that grief needs to be confronted and embraced right away and not allowed to build up internally. It has to be expressed, gotten out into the open. I was seeking a balance—I was not yet ready to tackle my grief head on, and I found that this short escape was just about right. This time away from "real life" to gain some balance and to examine and express emotions a little at a time was exactly what we needed.

David and Jennifer were sensitive in their conversation, seeming to understand that I needed to talk and to hear references to Leticia, but could not bear an entire week of eulogies. It was another coping mechanism: a release valve. I needed time away from the responsibilities of home and work, space before taking back the reins of my life. My emotions could not handle long tributes, but I needed to hear her name, to know that other people knew what I was thinking about. While I may not have shown it then, and for many months to follow, there was never a moment that I was not thinking about Leticia.

It was also the week of the first milestones. Not only had Leticia gone Home just before Christmas, but our anniversary and her birthday occurred that same week. Again, finding balance was crucial; I could not bear to make the whole day about Leticia, but I still wanted to mark these occasions in some way. On our anniversary I took one of the anniversary rings I had given her—one on our fifth, another on our tenth—out of the jewelry box and put it on my finger. I now wear it every day. On her birthday we followed our usual tradition and went to her favorite restaurant for dinner. No big ceremony, but an acknowledgment of her life.

And then there were two …
After New Year's Holden and I returned home. Following the hustle and bustle of the weekof the Honolulu funeral, the travel to the mainland, the Pasadena funeral, the San Francisco committal, and the days in Sacramento, the busyness suddenly ceased. After being surrounded by family, friends

and well–wishers, we were finally alone. It was time to face reality, to get back to work and school. This was the most difficult time of all. Just us ...

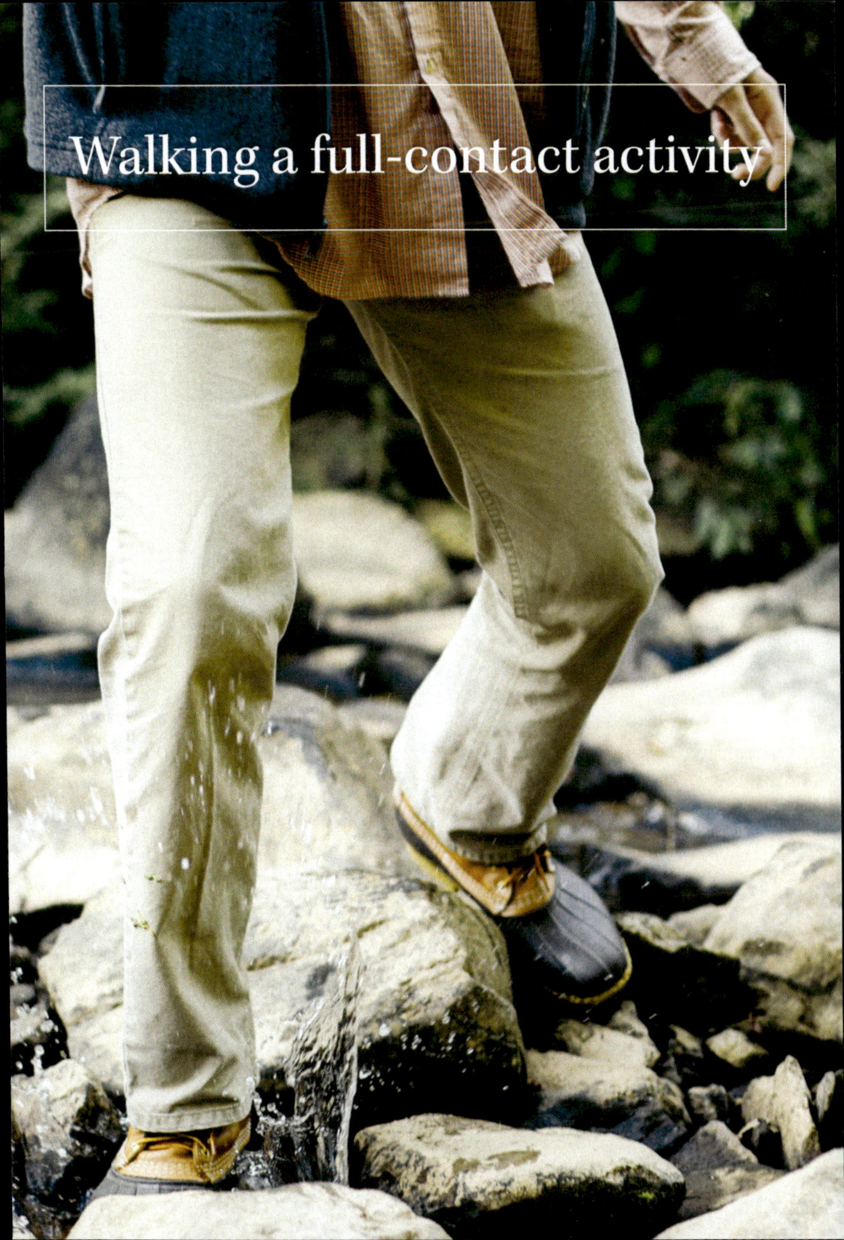
Walking a full-contact activity

"

In shock and denial, I covered

my emotions with work and

sought to deflect them by comforting

others and focusing on Holden.

"

FOUR

SUDDENLY I WAS EXHAUSTED—mentally, emotionally, and even physically. This surprised me, especially since I had given myself those days of rest and restoration in Sacramento. Turns out I needed much more than three short days. I found that I was not invincible. I needed to continue to rely on others to help me catch up and to give me space to grieve and to learn to be a single dad. Mostly, I needed to give myself permission to grieve.

Yet I also needed stimulation, a purpose, and a task at hand. So I headed back to work. There were Christmas reports to file, new programs to set up, and decisions to be made regarding Leticia's responsibilities. The weekly schedule beckoned: Sunday worship services, Bible studies, membership classes, youth programs, women's clubs, men's groups, teaching classes at the Army's Adult Rehabilitation Center, and more. For me, this was part of my therapy—putting this part of my life back together.

Because my ministry was inextricably tied to Leticia, it was both beneficial and emotionally difficult. Beneficial because it gave me additional opportunities to connect with her—finding replacements to handle her responsibilities and taking up the slack for functions she would no longer perform. Emotionally difficult because I saw her everywhere—each task was associated with her in some way. At the same time, I found this comforting because it allowed me to continue to have her in my thoughts, in a practical way, as I ensured that her programs and responsibilities continued. I could take the time to reflect and remember while still fulfilling my responsibilities and engaging in practical work.

My body was also under siege. With the public events now over, the adrenaline that had kept me going was bleeding off. The difficulty was that I did not want to go to bed. Despite being so very tired, both Holden and I realized that we were staying up later and later. We talked about it one night and realized it was for the same reason—we were avoiding getting into bed until we were sure we would fall asleep right away. Staying awake in bed meant being alone with our grief; our minds would automatically go to Leticia and the sadness would set in. So we stayed up until we could no longer keep our eyes open. Even then, it seemed that no matter how tired we were, sleep would not come.

My emotional self was in turmoil as well. This, of course, is expected and understandable. As a minister, I knew well the stages of grief made so famous by Elisabeth Kübler–Ross. I knew I had to get through "denial," "anger," "bargaining," and "depression" before I got to "acceptance." I knew it, and I also knew right where I was: denial. I knew it, but I did not believe it. How can you know something and still not believe it? How could I know I was in denial, yet not accept it? I knew that I knew. It was still so hard to comprehend that she was really gone, that she was not coming back. Analyzing one's own grief is surreal.

During those early weeks I displayed all the classic signs and phases of severe grief. In shock and denial, I covered my emotions with work and sought to deflect them by comforting others and focusing on Holden. So I would add another phase to Kübler–Ross's list: deflection. I had deflected dealing with "real life" by taking some time on the mainland. Now, I continued to deflect by jumping back into work.

Was it all a dream?

I could not believe that Leticia was really gone. I continued to wake up in the morning assuming it had all been a dream. Some mornings I would get as far as the bathroom before I realized that she was not waiting for me at the hospital. In typical grief mindset, I felt that if I ceased actively mourning for her, she would somehow be lost to history and that her memory would fade from existence. It was as if mourning her kept her close to me and kept her real in the world. I was not ready to let her go.

Holden and I talked about this one day. We had spent so long in the hospital—each night leaving her there and coming home alone—that we were already used to being home without Mom. Although I slept alone each night, when I awakened each morning, my first thought was to go and see Leticia at the hospital.

I knew that I had to allow my grief to surface, to deal with it and to let it manifest itself so that it in turn would lead to acceptance, but at the same time I knew I was not ready. I did not want that acceptance just yet. I saw myself moving from denial to something between depression and frustration with the very idea of acceptance. Acceptance would mean putting the past behind and "moving on." In a sense, it would mean leaving Leticia behind or, at least, putting less focus on her. I was not ready. My grief kept her alive, kept her memory strong in my mind.

C.S. Lewis and I

In *A Grief Observed* C.S. Lewis wrote that he felt he had to remain in grief for his wife as a way of staying connected to her. I can relate intimately with that feeling. To stop grieving was to let Leticia go. To stop thinking about her was to abandon her to history and to admit that she was gone. I wanted so badly for her to still be there that it was almost as if I believed I could think her back into existence. To stop doing so felt like abandonment and betrayal. How dare I cease thinking of her for even a minute? She deserved my total attention.

I have something else in common with C.S. Lewis. His wife's name was Helen Joy Davidman, but she went by the name Joy. "Leticia" is derived from the Latin word "laetitia," which means "joy." Lewis married Joy knowing she had cancer, knowing that their life together would be brief. I married Leticia knowing she had diabetes, knowing that I would likely outlive her.

After Joy died, Lewis was not afraid to yell at God—to kick and scream and demand answers. He remarked on his feeling of isolation: "There is a sort of invisible blanket between the world and me." For him, only Joy mattered. He didn't care about the rest of the world. He didn't even want to shave. "What does it matter now whether my cheek is rough or smooth?" he asked. What difference would his personal appearance make? He felt different from everyone else. He thought, *No one else understands; no one else has been through this; no one has loved as I did!*

And, like mine, his grief was total. "I not only live each endless day in grief, but live each day thinking about living each day in grief." Lewis found that grief fed on itself. The more he dwelled on it, the more all–consuming it became. Yet, he, like me, could do little to stem the tide. "Her absence is like the sky, spread over everything," he wrote. "I am thinking about her nearly always." He debated with himself whether the act of writing out his thoughts was helpful or just added to the pain: "It doesn't really matter whether you grip the arms of the dentist's chair or let your hands lie in your lap. The drill drills on."

From: Brian Saunders
To: Ivan Wild, Craig Bowler
Date: January 8, 2010, 2:14 AM
Re: Today

This sucks.

I've been a minister for almost 20 years. I've been a Christian for about as long as I can remember. I've never used bad language. I have a master's degree in theology. I have what I think is a fairly large vocabulary and pretty good communication skills. Yet the best phrase I can come up with for this is, "This sucks." Yes, I know "sucks" is a vulgar word. It is crude and demeaning, and the origins of its use do not bear consideration. But it pretty much sums up my feelings on Leticia's death. There is nothing good in this. No part of my life is better. No one will learn a lesson; no cause has been championed. No good will come of it.

My grief is all—encompassing. It surrounds and invades every part of my being: my thoughts, my emotions, my memories—even my body. Nothing is spared the agony of this loss. So, yeah, today, I'm using this word. This really does suck. The thing is, I know it's OK to say this right now. At least to you. It's all right—in fact, it's probably healthy to express my emotions. Even to God. God knows I'm mad. He knows I'm angry at Him. How dare He take Leticia! What's the plan, God? Where's the "all things work together for good for those who love God" in this? This is just bad all around. Why would He do this? I'm asking the questions, but getting no answers.

But God's got big shoulders. He can take it. I don't think He minds if His children sometimes tell Him what we really think. Anger is a perfectly acceptable emotion. And so is disappointment. Yes, God, I'm disappointed. Disappointed that You would choose this path for my family. I know You've got some perfect plan going on and that I'm supposed to trust You through the good times and the bad. And I do. But that does not mean I have to always like it—or that I even have to agree. And I don't like this, God. You should have chosen a different option here. This sucks.

God certainly knows how I feel. And I think He's OK with it. He'll let me have my tantrum. He knows I'll get through this night. Tomorrow, maybe I'll be more polite, more erudite and polished. My vocabulary and communications skills may kick in. But tonight, I just know it sucks.

Here is the insidiousness of grief: it affects everything. Every decision, choice, and action is considered through the prism of the memory of the deceased. It is not just "What would Leticia do?" but "How would she like it?" "What would her thoughts be?" "What would she say?" The world is just not right anymore. Nothing is. As Lewis put it, "There is spread over everything a vague sense of wrongness, of something amiss." He described it as suspense: "It gives life a permanently provisional feeling."

For Lewis, for me, for anyone who has experienced such loss, the pain is complete. No activity, action, or event is without it. Every corner of the mind, of the heart, of the body is hurting. It is as if you are in suspended animation: the rest of the world goes on; people get back to their normal lives; and the earth continues to revolve. But not for me. It feels like I am trapped between the past and the present. Longing to stay in the past, to dwell in the memories, to remember and recall so fiercely that, by some miracle, I can make those memories come alive again. Yet it cannot be. No matter what I say or do, her death is permanent. Irreversible. Leticia is never coming back.

From: **Brian Saunders**
To: **Ivan Wild, Craig Bowler**
Date: **January 11, 2010, 11:19 PM**
Re: **Today**

I read C.S. Lewis's book on the death of his wife last night. He describes losing her as like having an amputation. He's exactly right. It really is like losing a part of yourself. We always refer to spouses as "our better halves." Yeah, that's about right. It's at least half of me that's gone, and it's definitely the better half. The more faithful half. The wiser half. The more pastoral, spiritual, and creative half. I can't explain how hard it is to get used to it. Not sure I ever will. Not sure I want to. Lewis is right. That's exactly how I feel. Like I've been torn apart. A part is missing. It is just gone.

The thing is, once the limb is amputated the wound heals.

There are scars, but it heals. We can learn to live without it. We adapt and adjust. There are crutches and prostheses that help us get around. We can "make do" without the leg. But the leg will always be missing. It's not there anymore. Even the accommodations we create to adapt to it are a constant reminder of its loss. No matter what I do, no matter how I adapt, no matter what happens next, that leg is never going to be there. Not sure how to learn to walk again. But thanks for being my crutches.

Grieving as a family

My first priorities were to help Holden through his grief and to learn to be a single father. Holden was a 14–year–old boy, a teen going through all the normal adolescent changes, emotions, and conflicts. He was busy in school and in church and with friends. He didn't like to talk about his grief much. Yet he had matured so much during his mom's illness and death. I found that he needed space, but not quite enough space to allow him to completely avoid expressing his feelings. The car became a safe haven for discussions: if I brought something up, he could talk about it, knowing there was an end in sight—arrival at the destination. The car was a private place, and the trips were usually short, so they were a good opportunity for him to explore his feelings and gave him a chance to express his grief.

We took to cooking dinner together. This became another release valve for both of us and a good opportunity to spend time together. If our grief came up, we talked about it. Mostly, I allowed Holden to initiate the conversation. Deep–dish pizza—he makes a very good one—became our favorite, our "comfort food."

BULLETIN
January 4, 2010

Major Brian Saunders sends his thanks.

Dear Friends,

Holden and I would like to thank you for your support over the past several weeks following Leticia's promotion to Glory. We have been inundated with emails, cards and phone calls—in fact, we only finished reading through the cards last night. Thank you for the many comments, reflections, and stories about Leticia—they will be cherished. Most important, our deepest thanks for your prayers. We have felt a strength and a peace that far surpasses anything we have in ourselves, and we know it is God's care, through your prayers, that is carrying us through.

May God bless you each.

—Brian

One of the lessons I learned from Leticia is that family comes first. She was fiercely loyal to family. She once reminded me, "Holden and I will be the only members of this congregation that leave here with you." It was a lesson in priorities: No matter how hard you work for the people of any particular congregation, when you are transferred (as Salvation Army officers often are), they stay behind, but your family goes with you. While our ministry is to others, it includes our own family.

Grieving in a glass house

Life in a Glass House, by Cameron Lee and Jack Balswick, explores what it is like for ministers to raise a family. Grieving as a pastor's family, they say, is very much like grieving in a glass house. How true! Everyone could see us; we were very much on display day in and day out. As the corps officer, I was front and center every week. Holden was also very visible. I felt a responsibility to be a good role model for the congregation, but I also knew Holden's emotional and spiritual health were more important. Holden had to be my first priority, even if it meant shirking some duties occasionally. Sometimes, Holden and I would head off to the beach, or to a favorite restaurant for a while, just to be "alone," but not at home. At first I felt guilty—until I realized that there was nothing more important that I could possibly be doing.

A Final Report on Leticia: January 15, 2010

Dearest friends,

It's now been a month since Leticia went Home. I thought I'd send one last report—this one about Holden and me. …

Holden has grown immensely during these past few weeks and months. He has a strong faith and is absolutely sure of Mom's presence with God. Now that the public events are over, and it's just the two of us in the house, there are poignant moments—like when we made curry for the first time for dinner the other night, and both of us thought out loud, "Mom would love this!" A smile, a silence, a moment of reflection quickly passing. There will be many such moments in the coming months and years, and we are both aware that there will be difficult times ahead. But there are also joys. We spend a great deal of time together—we do just about everything as a team. (I'm not so sure Leticia would be quite so pleased with our frequent Nerf gun battles, but they do serve to bleed off the emotions.)

Naturally, we talk quite a bit about Heaven and eternal life. It is no longer just a euphemism to say that Mom has "gone Home" or "is in the arms of God"—it's personal, and it's real. I know that she is exactly where she has always wanted to be. While she was never fatalistic or morbid, Leticia always looked forward to being in Heaven. She understood in a deeply spiritual way that life on Earth—no matter how fulfilling—is just temporary, a mere instant in the scope of eternity. To say "she has gone Home" is exactly the right phrase for her. Home is where we belong, where we are most comfortable, where we can be real. She looked forward to getting on to her real life with God.

C.S. Lewis's *The Last Battle* portrays Judgment Day and the entrance of God's children into Heaven. "It was only the beginning of the real story. All their life in this world ... had only been the cover and the title page: now at last they were beginning Chapter One of the Great Story ... which goes on forever." That was Leticia's greatest hope and joy. I always enjoyed watching her sing her favorite hymns, the ones about Heaven. The final verse of "How Great Thou Art" says: "When Christ shall come with shout of acclamation/And take me home, what joy shall fill my heart!/Then I shall bow in humble adoration/And there proclaim 'My God, how great thou art!' " She would lift her head and close her eyes. A deep smile would come across her face. She would radiate love and anticipation as she sang. Her anticipation has become her reality.

Blessings upon you each.

Brian

Surrounded by our 'ohana'

A pastor does not live in a vacuum. A pastor is part of a community, a family within a family. In my case, that family was the Kauluwela Mission Corps "ohana" in Honolulu. Ohana is the word for family in Hawaiian. But the concept of ohana is deeper than just a biological relationship—it's about belonging and security. It's where you are welcomed unconditionally, where you feel comfortable and safe.

Even before Leticia went Home, our corps had become our ohana. During Leticia's illness, people brought dinner over to the house, did the yard work, and helped out at the corps. They were constantly calling and asking about her—always with a prayer and a smile. After her death, they wrapped Holden and me in a deep sense of belonging and support. Somewhere along the line, I ceased being just the officer and became one of the ohana. They ministered to me as I ministered to them.

Yet it didn't dawn on me at first that when Leticia died, our corps was in bereavement. I was focused on my own pain, and in trying to make things normal for everyone else, I did not notice that everyone else was grieving right along with me. My subconscious rationale was, "This is my tragedy; why bring everyone else down with me?" Flawed thinking, to be sure! The reality was that our entire corps was hurting. Not only did the officer lose his wife, the corps had lost its co-corps officer. And they had not lost just a leader; they had lost a friend.

The corps was in mourning. I saw it on their faces on Sunday mornings. Tears flowed at Leticia's name; memories and reflections abounded. I began talking about her more often in public and, once I felt I could do it, I shared in a sermon about her last days. I realized that my own tears as I spoke were not a sign of weakness at all, but a sign of strength—the willingness and courage to be vulnerable and honest with my ohana. In addition, it gave them permission to grieve themselves. They saw that the corps officer was OK with tears, so they were comfortable with them as well. That release was very important as it allowed us all to move through that phase of intense sadness and on to a more balanced grief. So we mourned as a church. We cried, we laughed, we shared. They continued to show incredible love and support in big ways and in small. I realized that I felt not so much like the leader, but like one of the family who happened to have the responsibility of preaching. We traveled the valley together.

One night after youth programs, I realized forcefully how much the people of the corps were grieving. I mentioned to Craig Rodriguera, our youth director, that we needed to clean the floor in the all–purpose hall. In particular, there was sticky residue in long lines across the floor where, months ago, Leticia had put tape to mark out the "yard lines" for an indoor football game. "We have to clean the tape marks up," I remarked.

"Can't we just leave it?" asked Craig. "It always reminds me of Major Leticia."

"Yeah," I said, "we can leave it for a while longer."

A lonely valley

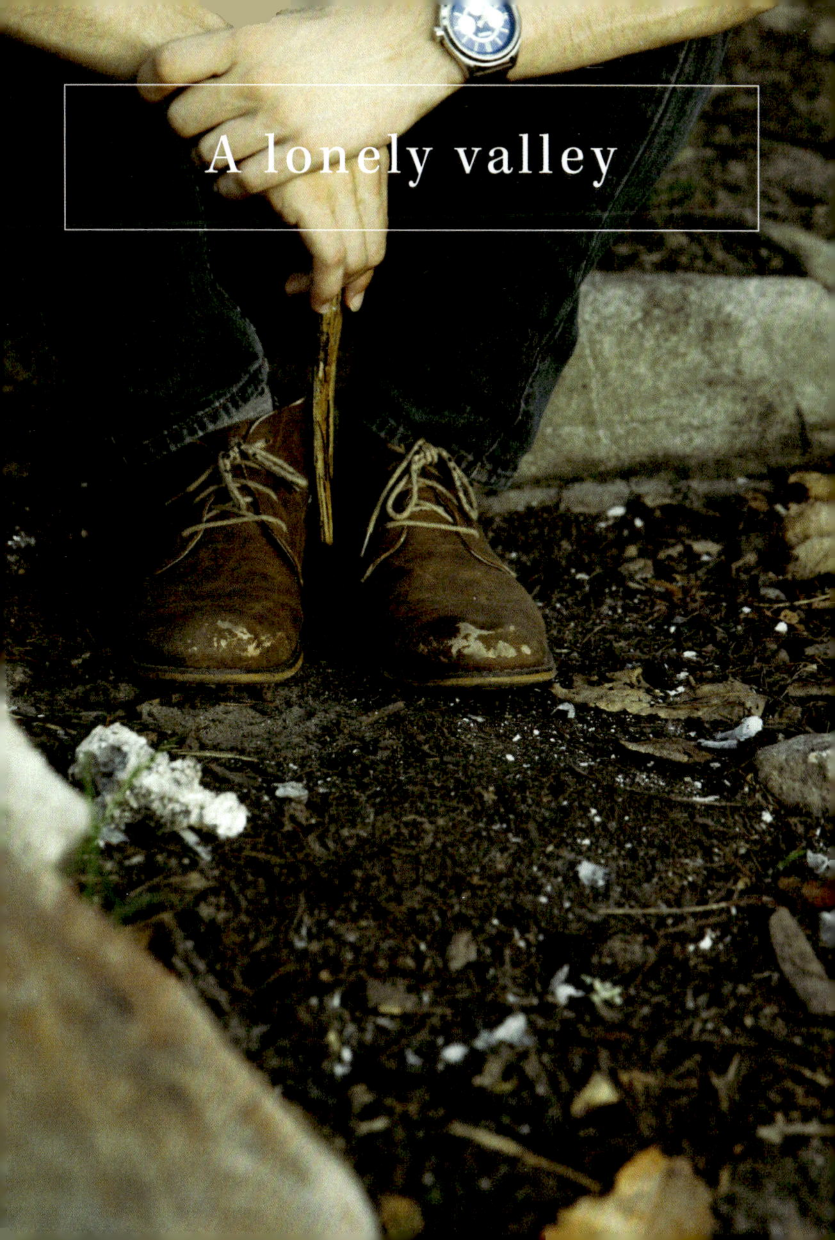

"

Nothing is the same; nothing
ever will be. She was my soulmate,
my lover, my home. The floor has
been snatched out from underneath
me and I am spinning out of
control into the abyss.

"

FIVE

From: Brian Saunders
To: Ivan Wild, Craig Bowler
Date: January 19, 2010, 3:02 PM
Re: Mahalo

OK, I know it's been a while, so the point is probably moot, but I still wanted to write an actual thank you note ...

Really, I can't express enough how much I appreciate you coming out here last month—and then of course coming back out to Pasadena and San Francisco. Looking back now, I can really appreciate how important that was—to be surrounded by my closest friends at the most difficult time in my life. Being able to laugh and share memories, to be distracted and yet also grieve, was a good balance. My folks are great, but I saw them as more "practical" support—it's both of you that I needed most. And of course, you were here. Thanks. Please make sure you tell Jennifer and Kristy I said thanks for letting you come as well—I know it took time away from your families. I guess this is where our ongoing discussion on the three cords comes in. I know that I am stronger because you guys are there—be it in person, via email, or over the phone. And Leticia's death is proof positive of the importance of our relationship—to have people around you ready to really come alongside in hard times is priceless and, unfortunately, all too rare. I've heard a few other people mention that they want to do similar things—to intentionally build up and cultivate a friendship for accountability and support—so perhaps our example will bear some other fruit.

So, Holden and I are getting used to our "new normal." It's going OK, but I confess it's harder than I thought it would be. (Ever read that "list of the most stressful life events"? "Death of a spouse" ranks #1—I understand why now.) As long as we are busy, it's OK, but we both have ups and downs. I think of Leticia constantly, and part of my brain still thinks she is just away on a long trip or still in the hospital. When something cool happens, I find myself thinking, "I can't wait to tell Leticia ..."; then, of course, it hits that I can't. And of course all these little accomplishments and cool moments will mean little to her (or me) when we do see each other again. I have finally started clearing out her stuff—I made it through the bathroom and her makeup table (why did she own five different hair dryers/curlers?). I figured out why I'm taking so long—apart from just being busy. I think it's about not being ready to clear her presence from the house—like getting rid of her stuff is in a way accepting the permanence of this, and taking away the evidence of her presence is in a way dismissing her from our lives, like she was never here. Not ready for that yet. Today after school we are going to clear out the "home office" and put our dining room back in place. So another step toward normalcy. I guess it's a good thing.

OK, thanks for letting me talk. I think writing must be cathartic for me. I hope you don't mind—I know you don't.

From:	**Craig Bowler**
To:	**Brian Saunders, Ivan Wild**
Date:	**January 19, 2010, 3:02 PM**
Re:	**Mahalo**

What a privilege to do life together. I am so grateful to be a part of both of your lives, and to walk out life and death together. Can't wait for the resurrection life together!

Brian, you mentioned about moving some of Leticia's things. There is a sacredness to such a move. To leave stuff alone reminds you of the past, but to move through these steps of putting things away helps to focus your attention on today, and on tomorrow. As you move Leticia's office, her makeup, and other things, know that you are just moving material things around. Leticia's memory and her legacy are not left in material things but in her spiritual qualities—in her grace, in her joy, in her hope, in her love. Those things can't be removed from your home. They will always be a part of your life, and those are the things that will be present in eternity.

A dad's journey ...

Leticia's only regret in leaving this Earth was that she would not get to see her son grow up. She loved him so deeply and so fiercely that only the hand of God Himself could have torn her away from him. They had a very close relationship. She had such plans and dreams for him. Holden loved her too. All his life he protected and helped her. He knew about low and high blood sugars and knew what to do when Mom's blood sugar was dropping. When Leticia was on dialysis before the kidney transplant, he studied the machines and understood how they all worked. During those last months in the hospital, he learned all he could about her various illnesses. He understood the equipment and medications and took time to sit and talk with Mom hour after hour.

As a dad, my main concern at Leticia's passing was Holden. My priority now was to protect his soul, to guard him against bitterness and anger toward God for taking his mother. My heart broke—it still breaks—each time I consider that he will grow up without knowing his mother. She will not share in any more milestones in his life, and he will not benefit from her wisdom and guidance. This is absolutely the hardest thing about her death.

So, how does a father grieve? How does he share that grief with his son? How does he help his son to understand and accept and—eventually—heal? I'm not sure I know the answer. I sought to deal with the grief early and head on, not shirking from it but talking about it openly and honestly.

Holden and I talked about Mom, gently and without getting too sentimental. We chose natural moments to talk about her, such as when we were eating something she liked or doing something that had some particular connection to her. Our little family has grown a bit smaller. Holden is now all I have, and I am all he has. We'll make it together.

From:	**Brian Saunders**
To:	**Craig Bowler, Ivan Wild**
Date:	**May 9, 2010, 11:39 PM**
Re:	**Mother's Day**

To be frank, this is not my favorite holiday. Here's the problem: It's the only holiday focused solely on the one thing that is glaringly missing in our lives. Mother's Day is all about moms. It's a great opportunity to recognize our mothers, to show appreciation for all their hard work and loving care. But when that one person has been torn away from the family, the day becomes a stark reminder of the loss. The commercials in the weeks before Mother's Day are relentless; church services are thematic; and everyone is greeting each other with "Happy Mother's Day." This is all good and appropriate, something I wouldn't discourage in a million years. But it's not a good day for me.

So, I have a confession: For the whole day, I forgot I had a mom. It's true. (And I'm very sorry, Mom!) My emotions today were all about Holden and me. My Mother's Day was wrapped around my son's mother and the terrible reality that he will never celebrate Mother's Day with his mom again. He will never make her breakfast in bed, never send her a card, never forget to call when he has a family of his own. How does a kid deal with watching everyone else celebrate when he is lacking the one thing being celebrated? Christmas and other holidays are different—at least the focus is on something else, something we can still participate in. Not so with Mother's Day. So my heart is breaking once again, for both of us.

And now I feel guilty. With all my focus on my wife, I forgot my own mother! Not good. But I know she understands. Leticia's mom passed away at the hands of a drunk driver over 20 years ago. Once, early in our marriage, Leticia related that story to my mother, saying how much she missed her. My mom took Leticia's hand, and said simply, "I can't be your mother, but I can love you like one." I suppose the same is true now. Holden may not have a mom, but he has a wonderful grandmother, someone who loves him deeply and will always be there for him.

Mother's Days will get better. I'm learning to separate those deep, long-term emotions from the activities of the day. Holden and I can still celebrate Mother's Day. We can't bring her breakfast in bed, but we can say a prayer of thanks for her, and remind each other how much she meant—and continues to mean—to us.

A husband's steps ...

In the introduction to *A Grief Observed*, Douglas H. Gresham, C.S. Lewis's adopted son, says, "All human relationships end in pain. It is the price that our imperfection has allowed Satan to extract from us for the privilege of love." Lewis himself wrote, "Bereavement is a universal and integral part of our experience of love."

To love is to be vulnerable—to the loved one, to the world around us, to God Himself. We put ourselves in harm's way when we love someone. To love is also to lose. The " 'til death us do part" is a reality in every marriage. Someone will die first. We know it going in; yet, in our youthful naiveté, we choose to ignore it. Even Leticia and I—who had talked frankly and openly about her life expectancy as a diabetic—were not prepared for her death. So how do you grieve as a spouse?

Throughout this grieving process I automatically sought to comfort and bring assurance to others—Holden first, of course, and then the corps. That's all well and good, but at the center of it all is simply me. Not Major Brian Saunders, the Salvation Army officer, Major Brian the pastor, or even Dad—just Brian, the husband. Brian, the man who lost his wife. This is hard. My wife is dead. How do I deal with that? Every single area of my life is now irrecoverably different. Nothing is the same; nothing ever will be. She was my soulmate, my lover, my home. The floor has been snatched out from underneath me and I am spinning out of control into the abyss.

That's what it felt like. Surrounded by friends and family, I felt totally isolated, completely alone. That's another characteristic of grieving: loneliness. Grief feels like being adrift in a rowboat on the ocean. At best, the sea is calm; there is a peace and serenity that surrounds and encompasses you. At worst, a storm comes and you are battered by the wind and tossed by the waves. Either way, you are alone.

That was me. No one understood; no one *could* understand, not because they were not trying, but simply because none of them had ever experienced anything like this. Grief causes self–centeredness and myopic thinking. Of course I knew that many, many others—even people I knew—had experienced loss. But this was *my* pain. I was looking inward; seeing others only as *not me.* Their world would go on, pretty much the same. Mine was forever changed. I was alone.

Yet, even in the darkest valley, I knew Someone was there with me.

Stepping out in faith...

In *A Grief Observed*, C.S. Lewis described his anger and frustration with God as his wife's body was ravaged by cancer. "Month by month and week by week You broke her body on the wheel whilst she still wore it." It is the age–old question: Why does God allow suffering? Why did God put Joy, her children, and C.S. Lewis through this? Why did He put

Leticia, Holden, and me through this? Lewis says exactly what so many of us have thought: "Not that I am (I think) in much danger of ceasing to believe in God. The real danger is of coming to believe such dreadful things *about* Him." (italics mine)

I can relate to Lewis. I can believe and have faith in God, sure, but He certainly tests my love for Him when He treats me like this. How can we *not* question God when such things happen? It is one thing to fret over random violence or natural disasters; it is quite another when tragedy strikes home. Where is He when I need Him?! We lash out at God, rail against his seemingly senseless and arbitrary decisions. "You say You make all things work together for the good of those who love you. What good could possibly come of this? What grand purpose could this serve?" We raise our arms, clenching our fists as we shout out to the heavens, "What's the good in this, God?" We sob out a whisper as we weep, "Why God, why?" We want to know the answer to the age-old question. Job asked it; the Psalmist asked it; Lewis asked it; I asked it. I still ask it. "Why?"

I have not received an answer. No voice from Heaven, no sign from on high signaling a God who cares. No relief, no indication of a grand scheme, no evidence that it will all indeed work out for good. Silence. Darkness.

How do we reconcile our idea of a loving, personal God with a God that would allow such heartbreak? Do we believe in the vengeful, judgmental God of the Old Testament, or the loving, sacrificial God of the New Testament? There is tension here—we live in it every day. In another of C.S. Lewis's books, *The Lion, The Witch and the Wardrobe,* he casts Aslan the lion in the role of God. "Is he safe?" asks Lucy. "Safe?" replies Mr. Beaver. "Who said anything about safe? 'Course he isn't safe. But he's good."

Yes, God is good. God is, after all, God. To be God, He must be good. He is the great sovereign, Lord of all creation. King of Kings and Lord of Lords. He is omniscient and omnipotent. He holds the fate of the universe in His hands. So, no, he's not "safe," but He is good. He can be trusted because He is all of the above. Lord and Lover. Sovereign and Father. He knows all. And He knows me. That's why I can trust Him—no matter what.

So, as I walk through this dark valley, I find, with the Psalmist, that I'm not afraid. I know God is with me. Somehow, I just know. The Shepherd walks alongside. I will fear no evil—because He is with me. Silent perhaps, but always present. Yet maybe—just maybe—not so silent. Maybe I do hear him—in the soft encouragement of friends, in the acts of kindness and love of family, the arm around a shoulder, the quick pat on the back. I hear Him speak through His Word. In Scripture, I see pictures of the Kingdom of Heaven—of comfort, peace, and ultimate joy. I hear Him when I pray, not when I speak, but when I listen—that still, small voice, reminding me that He is indeed here.

That's what faith is—accepting, trusting what we cannot see, what we do not understand. I can have faith in God—even that God is good—even through bad times. Even my anger at God, my shouting and questioning, indicates faith. I would not shout at Him if I didn't believe in Him. So, yes, I'm mad at God. Yet I can still claim Him as God—my God, my Shepherd, and my companion. Perhaps that's what being a believer is all about.

During those early weeks, I spent a great deal of time praying. I prayed for Holden, for our corps, for me. I prayed for Leticia's legacy, for God to bless it. Sometimes I shouted at God. I yelled at Him and questioned why He would take Leticia. At other times, prayer became a solace—a soothing time when I could dwell on Leticia while at the same time releasing her to God. The good news was that God was already answering those prayers by surrounding me with people who filled my life with support, encouragement, and love. Just knowing that they were there, that they were seeking to understand, wanting nothing more than to ease my pain—even a little bit—was like a light shining through the darkness, a helping hand along the treacherous road.

From: Craig Bowler
To: Brian Saunders, Ivan Wild
Date: February 13, 2010, 5:33 AM
Re: Thoughts

You mentioned you wanted some stuff for a scrapbook. Here are my thoughts ...

Leticia Adams Saunders was *convinced*. I met Leticia in about 1990. I met her as your friend, Brian. I don't recall if she was your girlfriend at the time, or if you guys were still checking each other out. I think you might have been more convinced at the time about her than she was about you, but that would soon change. It would soon be evident to all that Leticia was as *convinced* about you as you were about her.

As the next year unfolded you guys became more and more *convinced* that life and ministry would be done together. Your hearts were united around the cause of Christ and the call to officership. And off you went to change the world. *Convinced* that above all else, Christ would be glorified. He was, and He is.

I only got to be with Leticia on occasion. Those occasions were all so full of life, sometimes debate, and even sacredness. Our year of training school together, your commissioning, your wedding, visiting us on our first assignment, Holden's dedication, your transplant, moves to England, Salem [Oregon], etc. There was always a trust and hope in something greater. Leticia never seemed to doubt. As a person of doubt myself, I always admired that character trait.

Leticia always seemed certain. She seemed strong. She was *convinced*.

Holden came along and this trait was fortified. Holden, being the In—N—Out Burger lover that he is, was always so close to Leticia's heart. Leticia loved you, Holden, with a unique love. Your conversations with your mom were always so different than the conversation that I have with my girls. You guys talked about Shakespeare and rockets and creation. My kids talk about soccer, the Disney Channel, and makeup. It's not that your mom loved you more than I love my girls, but your mom loved you in a way that is unique to you and your mom. See, your mom was *convinced* that you were a gift of God to her and your dad. She was *convinced* that God uniquely put you together. He wired you up for something great. He wired you up not to just hang out at the burger stand, but to soar above the challenges of this world, and the challenges of this day. Your mom was *convinced* that you were her beloved. You are her beloved son, and with you, Holden Saunders, your mom is well pleased.
But most of all I know that Leticia was *convinced* of her faith and trust in her Savior. Her heart for Him was bigger, deeper, and wider than just about anyone's I know. I don't think I ever saw or heard about Leticia being afraid. She was so at home in the arms of her Savior. Leticia was convinced that her Savior could conquer any disease, any trial and challenge of this world, and that one day He would move her to the eternal. Her faith is now fact. How *convinced* is she now?

I read this passage at Leticia's interment service. I think it's absolutely true of Leticia's life, death, and her resurrection in Christ.

"No, in all these things we are more than conquerors through him who loved us. For I am *convinced* that neither death nor life, neither angels nor demons, neither the present nor the future, nor any powers, neither height nor depth, nor anything else in all creation, will be able to separate us from the love of God that is in Christ Jesus our Lord." (Romans 8:37–39, italics added)

From: **Brian Saunders**
To: **Ivan Wild, Craig Bowler**
Date: **March 31, 2010, 10:08 PM**
Re: **Thanks**

Hey,
just a quick note to say thanks for your part in our vacation along with some thoughts ...

Ivan, thanks for letting us stay at your house. Fun times with Chelsea and Keegan. As I said, I have not been to two movies in one weekend since high school! It was great to go to Disneyland too. And to stay in the Disney Hotel—one of Leticia's "bucket list" items. Craig, thanks for making the contact for the tours in Washington. And thanks for coming up. It was good to see you so soon, and good to see Holden interacting with you so well. Cool.

As I anticipated, this trip was a bit bittersweet. Good times, but hard as well. Leticia had always wanted to see Washington, D.C. She especially thought it was important for Holden to visit the Air and Space Museum and was really looking forward to taking him there. There were poignant moments—especially at the Library of Congress, knowing how much Leticia loved books and reading. The grief bubbled to the surface as I took in the massive collection of tomes. My first thought whenever something cool happens is "I can't wait to tell Leticia … " I really wished she could have been there and seen what I was seeing. At the same time, I realized—or perhaps God brought it to me—that these things really don't matter to her anymore. All these things that seemed so important—seeing the Declaration of Independence, going to the Library of Congress, staying at the Disneyland Hotel—are inconsequential to her now. She does not mind not having seen them, since her reality is so much greater than ours. It's a helpful thought, although the grief is still there. Overall, I'd describe the trip as more "important" than "fun." (People keep asking me if I had fun on vacation—not sure how to answer.) It was a good trip and included fun times and laughs.

Washington was inspirational and educational, and Disney was enjoyable, but it was not really "fun" in the traditional vacation way. It was, however, an important experience—important that we got out there and did something. Important that we went ahead with Leticia's trip without her. It will make the next trip easier as we get used to life without her.

It's now been three and a half months. There is no "timeline" for grief, but we are definitely in a valley period. The permanency is settling in and it's much harder than I had anticipated. Someone the other day said they could not imagine what I was going through. I said I would not even want them to try.

Even trying to imagine what one's life would be like without your spouse is very painful. And unless it's real, it's impossible to really imagine.

I can't sing most worship songs through—especially any of Leticia's favorites, all of which seem to be about Heaven. It's a good feeling to hear them; it makes me feel close to Leticia but makes me sad at the same time. I think my major concern right now is Leticia's legacy. The rest of the world has moved on, and I'm not ready—and there is this fear that everyone else has forgotten about her. (Yes, I know that's irrational, but it's also a normal part of grieving.)

The Youth Councils theme ("Identity") has made me think about how I identify myself, and what labels the world uses to describe who I am. I used to be a husband, a married officer, a partner—parent, a co—corps officer. Now my labels are different: single parent, single officer, corps officer. Suddenly, I'm not who I was. It's a bit of a thought—stopper. I'm someone different. I am labeled differently. I am even paid differently. But then, I think about the labels that have not changed: dad, friend, brother, and most important, child of God. None of that has changed. I'm deeply grateful that I get to hold on to these. If we are defined by our relationships, then this is who I am now. OK, thanks as always for letting me express like this. It's good for me.

Brian

From: **Craig Bowler**
To: **Brian Saunders, Ivan Wild**
Date: **April 5, 2010, 7:07 AM**
Re: **Re: thanks**

Thanks for the note Brian. …

Love the identity stuff you've been thinking about. I saw your usage of the word *labels* and it made me think of some of the stuff we've been writing here. Jesus Loves You, Everyone Else Thinks You Are a _____ . Whatever goes in the blank is the label. But at the end of the day, as you said, you are a child of God. You are His Beloved. You are His son and He loves you. Label or no label. You are His. …

Looking forward to Spring Break here! Today is a beautiful day in Atlanta. Adele and I are headed to an afternoon Braves baseball game. Can't wait!

cb

In *A Resilient Life*, Gordon MacDonald makes a case for "writing out the elements of [your] life in order to drain them of all the wisdom they have to offer." I was unknowingly doing this from the very beginning: documenting Leticia's ministry in the hospital, sharing her progress with others, and using it all to honor her and deal with my grief at the same time. I frequently write to Craig and Ivan. The letters are not really for them at all—they are for me, a way to express my feelings in security. It doesn't matter whether they respond—in fact, I often remind them that no response is needed—what's important is that I have an outlet for my feelings. It doesn't matter where I am or what time it is, I can always send off a quick note on my laptop or phone.

From:	**Brian Saunders**
To:	**Undisclosed Recipients**
Date:	**April 14, 2010, 7:06 PM**
Re:	**Four Months**

Dear Friends,

So, today is four months since Leticia's death. Time to write another missive ...

One thing I've learned in recent years is that it is OK to have feelings, and it is necessary to acknowledge them, allow them to be expressed (obviously, another of Leticia's many influences). It may sound weird since it comes so naturally to some people, but it took me a long time to understand that feelings are real and important and can't just be swept under the carpet all the time. That's the way it was in my family—no arguments, no raised voices, not even much in the way of expressed emotion, although of course all those things were there. So, coming together with someone from Leticia's background meant I had to learn that it was OK to say what I think, and to stand up for what I believe. So, jump to the present: Now I'm in that place where I need to express my feelings, and let the grief come, and even express my frustrations to God. Grief is real and tangible and affects virtually everything. Nothing is as easy or fun as it used to be. Everything is harder, and more melancholy. The thing, of course, is to balance that with faith, hope, and internal joy. To "live above feelings." We can go ahead and have—and express—our feelings but choose to carry on despite them. They need to be acknowledged and included, but they don't have to rule. I think that's part of the grieving process—moving on while still allowing those feelings to be a part of who you are. Not sure if any of that makes sense, but there you go.

Decisions: Another element that I have been mulling over: I find it harder—and easier—to make decisions. Over the past 20 years, I had gotten accustomed to deferring to Leticia on decisions and judgment calls (whether she believed it or not!). I relied on her discernment, knowledge, and, obviously, her style and creativity. I used her as my sounding board and final judgment on just about everything. But now I have to make decisions on my own. Yesterday it was as simple as what color would look best for some new certificates for the church. I automatically thought, *Leticia would know* ... This happens every day. I also find myself asking, *What would Leticia do?* (I know, it sounds a bit blasphemous!) So, another thing that is harder now. But, of course, in a way, it's also easier because I can stand by her convictions, and in so doing, honor her, and continue her legacy—even if no one else knows it. I can make quick work of decisions by simply thinking, *OK, that's what Leticia would do.*

Kidney: I had another random thought the other day. (Again, I don't know that these are of any importance, but it is definitely helpful to me to write them out, so bear with me....) My kidney is gone forever; burned to dust and buried in the ground in San Francisco. Now, I know that's obvious, and it wasn't like I was going to get it back anyway, but I guess it was always nice to be able to look over at Leticia and know that my kidney was there, working hard, keeping her alive. Not that I really thought about it all that much, but I guess it's part of that "absence makes the heart grow fonder" thing—even with your own kidney.

Worship services: I have come to really enjoy—and dread—our evening worship services. Our "Upper Room" service is contemporary, run by Rob Noland. We sing for half an hour, then Rob, a guest, or I teach. After the meeting we linger for a while, then head to the streets of downtown Honolulu to hang out with the homeless, the prostitutes, and the drug addicts. The service is typically contemporary. I like the simplicity and the music. I like the energy and enthusiasm, and I am very proud of our young people as they deepen their relationship with God and demonstrate their commitment through the outreach ministry. They are fired up! But I also find that I cannot get through a service without tears. I always think about Leticia and singing worship songs—one of her favorite things to do. Remember in "Chariots of Fire" how Eric Liddell said, "When I run, I feel God's pleasure"? Leticia felt God's pleasure when she worshiped. She would tilt her head back, close her eyes, and sing with this big smile on her face. As close to Heaven as you can get. So the good news is that during the service I get caught up in how much like Heaven this must be, and how much Leticia must be enjoying it; the bad news is that it makes me miss her that much more.

Holden made another important comment last night. He is going to the Robotics National Championships in Dallas next month. He found out that one of his heroes, Grant from "MythBusters," is going to be there. He immediately said he wished Mom could have known, since she always said that Holden was so much like Grant and that he could be successful and innovative just like him. There will be many moments like that. Normal life is hard and, of course, special events are even harder. Still, we allow for feelings, and move through, despite them.

So, at four months, life marches on. Today I have a funding grants meeting, and then a budget meeting. This afternoon is youth and corps programs. At 3:40, the time of Leticia's death, I will be picking up kids. But my heart and my mind will be with her.

Thanks for listening.

Brian

Real and abstract loss

I have an analytical mind. Even as I have been traversing this valley, I have examined my own footprints. Experts tell us that focusing on what exactly was lost is a key to facing it. By categorizing loss, we tame it and sort out how to deal with it. For example, is the loss "real" or "abstract"? In the case of the death of a spouse, the loss is both "real" and "abstract." It is "real" in the sense that there is a tangible loss of a partner. It is abstract in that it involves the loss of intangibles such as love and support.

I have lost the person with whom I shared physical tasks and responsibilities—both at home and at work. Leticia and I were partners in every sense of the word—a team both at home and work. I relied on her for so many aspects of the partnership.

At work, she was responsible for programming and pastoral care. Leticia led the weekly women's ministries and oversaw children's programs. She taught music classes and Girl Guards and organized dinner for the community kids who came for the after-school programs. She handled the corps paperwork. She was the creative director, often doing artwork and writing scripts for plays and musicals. She was great at coming up with games and activities for kids' programming; our usual routine was that she would come up with the ideas and get everything ready and organized, and I would lead the program itself.

We shared the pulpit, taking turns preaching every other week; when the corps had two services, one of us preached in the morning, the other in the evening. We worked on the preaching/teaching calendar together, but she was always the one who thought of creative alliterated titles and themes. She took care of the kitchen and organized all the special events. She enjoyed making the dining room look festive for special occasions and was a great decorator. She even liked coming up with new ways to fold the linen napkins for formal dinners!

At home we divided household chores pretty evenly. We partnered in parenting as well, always making decisions together, although she often took the lead. When he was 6, Holden was diagnosed with Asperger's Syndrome, and Leticia was the one who organized his doctor visits and counseling. She advocated for him at school and made sure that he was adapting well to each new class. She was usually the one who helped Holden with his homework and school projects. (Let's be honest, his intelligence quickly outstripped mine; he needed Mom's smarts!)

To be sure, the loss of a spouse is a real, physical loss. But the psychological loss is no less real. Leticia made decisions quickly and forcefully. I could always rely on her for an opinion or a judgment call, and I relied on her counsel both at work and at home. She was a support and a sounding board. Her instincts were very good. She had the spiritual gift of discernment, which was a blessing in the business and ministry aspects of our work, as well as at home. She was direct and secure in her decisions.

Leticia's determination was often a key factor in negotiations with donors and contractors. Once, when we were building the Ray & Joan Kroc Corps Community Center in Salem, Oregon, we were being pressured by the community and political leaders to move the chapel off to the side of the building, away from the "community" facilities. There was a great deal of discussion and weighty comments by stakeholders. Leticia looked around the table at all these powerful and influential people and said calmly, "The chapel will be in the center, and the Cross will be the highest structure." Because we were transferred away from Salem before construction was complete, Leticia did not live to see the new building with her own eyes, but I am proud to say that I have been there and I have seen the chapel at the center of the community center, with the Cross standing high above the massive building. Just as Leticia had said.

Suddenly, I am without those gifts, those contributions to my life. In my case, the phrase, "my better half" is no empty flattery or eulogy. It is a fact. Leticia was the creative, talented one in our partnership. She was the one with the rock–solid backbone, the conviction on what is right and the courage to see it through. My skills and gifts are far more plebean.

I now have to cover for her responsibilities and programs at work. I have to lead by myself. I have to take care of the house and our son on my own. I have to make decisions without the benefit of her wisdom and strength. But I find myself thinking more like her. Things that were important to her have now become my interests, and her soapboxes mine. Even on things that we may have disagreed on, I find myself advocating for her position.

The loss of Leticia is real indeed. It is also abstract. An abstract loss is one that is intangible—something ethereal but nevertheless affecting real emotions, which are harder to fix. These are the scars that will not heal, the limb that will not grow back. I had known Leticia for 20 years. In that time we fell in love, got married, had a child, traveled the world on behalf of The Salvation Army, and took on postings and responsibilities far beyond my talents and abilities. In every way possible, our lives were inextricably entwined. I had been with her my entire adult life, and I know no other mode of existence. I have lost love, companionship, mutual support, and encouragement. These are things I simply can't replace.

To: Craig Bowler, Ivan Wild
Date: May 12, 2010, 11:18 PM
Re: Today

I filled out an online form today. I came to the line for "marital status." The choices were: "single," "married," "divorced," and "widowed." Didn't like it at all. Of all the new labels I have to endure, I dislike this one the most. Why can't it just be "single" and "married?" Why do they have to point out the reason I am now single? What difference does it make? I get it; I'm single. I certainly don't want to be single. And honestly, I don't feel single. I feel very much married. To me, it feels like Leticia is very much a part of me, even though she's not here with me.

That's the way I like it. The other day I picked up one of the la-dies for Home League. She said she was glad I was still young and that she was sure I would find someone soon. I swear, I almost kicked her out of the car! I know she was just trying to be nice and to help me see forward. But come on!

I really hate the label "widower." It's too much of a reminder, like a poke in the emotional eye. It's like a neon sign saying, "Hey, this guy is different; he's lonely, he's hurt. Feel sorry for him." I feel alone enough already. No need to keep pointing it out.

Anyway, that's today's rant. Thanks for listening.

Love you guys.

To:	Ivan Wild, Craig Bowler
Date:	May 13, 2010, 11:48 PM
Re:	Identity

Some new thoughts rolling around my brain tonight. I do not like the new labels I wear: "single" and "widower." I see myself as the same person I always have been—part of a couple, the "Brian" half of "BrianandLeticia." I said I still feel married. All that is still true. The new wrinkle is about the passage of time. The more time passes, the more new people will come into my life—people who did not know Leticia and do not know me as half of a couple. I don't like the idea of being known with-out Leticia as part of my identity. I don't want people to know me apart from Leticia. I know it's inevitable. I know that I was always my own person even when Leticia was alive. Still, my identity was enmeshed with hers. Now, people are beginning to know me as just "Brian." It's OK for now, but what about 10, 20 years from now? What will Leticia's role in my life be? When people see me, will they recognize Leticia's role in my history, or will they see just me? I suppose it's up to me. Part of legacy, part of recognizing who I am.

It goes without saying that Leticia and I loved each other. Love is the greatest of human emotions, but it is also so comprehensive as to almost defy categorization. To say "I have lost love," is to say I have lost companionship, support, a sense of belonging and security. I have lost physical contact and intimacy, emotional security, and wise counsel. I have lost my sounding board and filter, the one whom I could bounce ideas off without fear of rejection or scorn, the one who would gently (usually!) sift through my thoughts to find the right direction to go. She was also the one to whom I could vent my frustrations and anger. She would support me and back me up no matter what, but she was also there to help filter my reactions—to make sure my responses were appropriate and beneficial. I needed her in so many ways.

Where's the tour guide?

So I come to the age-old question: "Where is God when we

hurt?" Grief feels like abandonment. Losing Leticia was like that; my hiking buddy had disappeared, and so, it seemed, had everyone else—including God. Lewis asked the question: "But go to him when your need is desperate, when all other help is vain, and what do you find? A door slammed in your face, and a sound of bolting and double bolting on the inside. After that, silence."

Silence. It smothers and covers me. It is oppressive; sometimes it feels as if I cannot breathe. I want Him to say something, to make His presence known, to offer comfort and hope. So where is God? He's here, right here, in the silence. That's God. He's not mouthing clichés or bringing over casseroles. But He's there. Perhaps I can't hear Him. But I can know Him.

So where is God when we hurt? He's closer than ever. God loves us. He knows us, and he knows our pain. This all–powerful, all–knowing, all–feeling God lives right here with us, in the very pain that can make us feel as if He is so far away. Psalm 139:5 reminds us: "You hem me in—behind and before; you have laid your hand upon me." If we draw closer to God when we are in pain, He draws closer to us. It's certainly not easy to recognize in the moment, but once we come to that realization, it makes the journey that much more bearable. Where is God when we hurt? Right beside us.

April 14, 2010

Where Are You?

Dearest Leticia,

It's been four months. Outwardly, things are falling into a routine. We are getting used to our "new normal." We are learning to deal with life differently. But I've been starting to ask questions—at least to myself. Yes, I know I'm a minister. I have a degree in theology, and I've read lots of texts on eschatology and the after–life. I know what the Bible says and what various scholars and theologians theorize about heaven, angels, and humans in eternal life. But sometimes I just want to know something simple: Where are you?

What do you know, what can you feel? Do you know what's happening on Earth, right now? Is the New Heaven and New Earth happening already; out of time and space? Or are you in some kind of out–of–time existence, waiting for Judgment Day when we will all arrive together? Where are you? I mean, where are you right now, in my context? It's a good question. Or is it? If time is relative and has no meaning outside the physical universe, then the question itself is nonsensical. The time/space continuum only has four dimensions, and if you are in none of them, then in what form do you exist? Even asking the question, "Where are you now?" makes no sense. There is no "now" for you. C.S. Lewis talked about this in *A Grief Observed.* He asked the same question: "Where is she now? That is, in what place is she at the present time?" He attempted no answer, but posed the deep question: "If the dead are not in time, or not our sort of time, is there any clear difference, when we speak of them, between *was* and *is* and *will be*?"

There are lots of eschatological theories and theologies. Postmillennial, amillennial, pre–tribulation, post–tribulation. There are those who suggest a kind of purgatory—like a heavenly waiting room. Others claim to have gone and come back, reporting a "great light" and a tunnel. Some say Judgment Day is an individual event; we walk up to Peter at the Pearly Gates one by one. Others suggest it will be a universal judgment, when the sheep are separated from the goats. Some will be granted access to heaven; others will be condemned to hell. This is not an eschatological treatise. So, I just ponder the simplest form of the question: Where are you? Right now, in my time/space continuum? How do you and I relate in this moment as I sit here at this table in Honolulu tonight? There are no answers. Just questions. And really, it's not a question. Since I know the question itself is nonsense. Location has no meaning, no basis outside the created universe. You are not here. As humans we look to the sky, and think of Heaven as "up there." But that's not where you are. People say things like, "She'll always be present in your heart." True enough—as far as it goes. My memory of you, my emotions toward you, your opinions and legacy will indeed remain a part of my personality. But you are not actually here. I wish you were.

No matter how it is analyzed or categorized, the bottom line is that the loss of a spouse is devastating. It is a total loss, putting the survivor into a tailspin. In losing Leticia, I lost the one person in the world closest to me. So Leticia's death has affected and changed every single part of my life.

I have heard comments like "God will help you through this," and "You are going through a difficult time" often in the past months. I admit to becoming frustrated with the word "through." This valley has no exit. Leticia is not coming back. I will travel in this valley for the rest of my life. It's not about "getting through"; it's about adapting and getting used to my new life. This is who I am now, a traveler through a valley not of my choosing. Nothing is the same; little is recognizable. Each milestone and marker is seen and felt a little differently, with a little less joy and a bit more melancholy. Still, I know that one day, the valley will not be so deep. I will always be journeying through it, but it won't always be quite so arduous a journey.

Throughout these months, I have come to understand Kübler–Ross's stages of grief at a much deeper level. I would contend that they are not so much "stages" as they are "phases," and that they are not so much chronological as they are interchangeable. I experience several of these emotions in any given week—or even in a day. They continue to come and go in no particular order. I understand that over the course of time, a person gradually comes to a sense of "acceptance"; however, the timeline does not proceed in an orderly manner or according to any predetermined set of rules. The emotions continue to swirl—just when you think you have "moved on" to the next stage, an older emotion comes to the fore. You bounce back and forth, experiencing the same feelings over and over, with little sense of movement toward a positive resolution.

C.S. Lewis put it well: "For in grief nothing 'stays put.' One keeps on emerging from a phase, but it always recurs. Round and round. Everything repeats. Am I going in circles, or dare I hope I am on a spiral?" The question, for Lewis, and for me: Is this spiral going up or going down?

A bend in the road

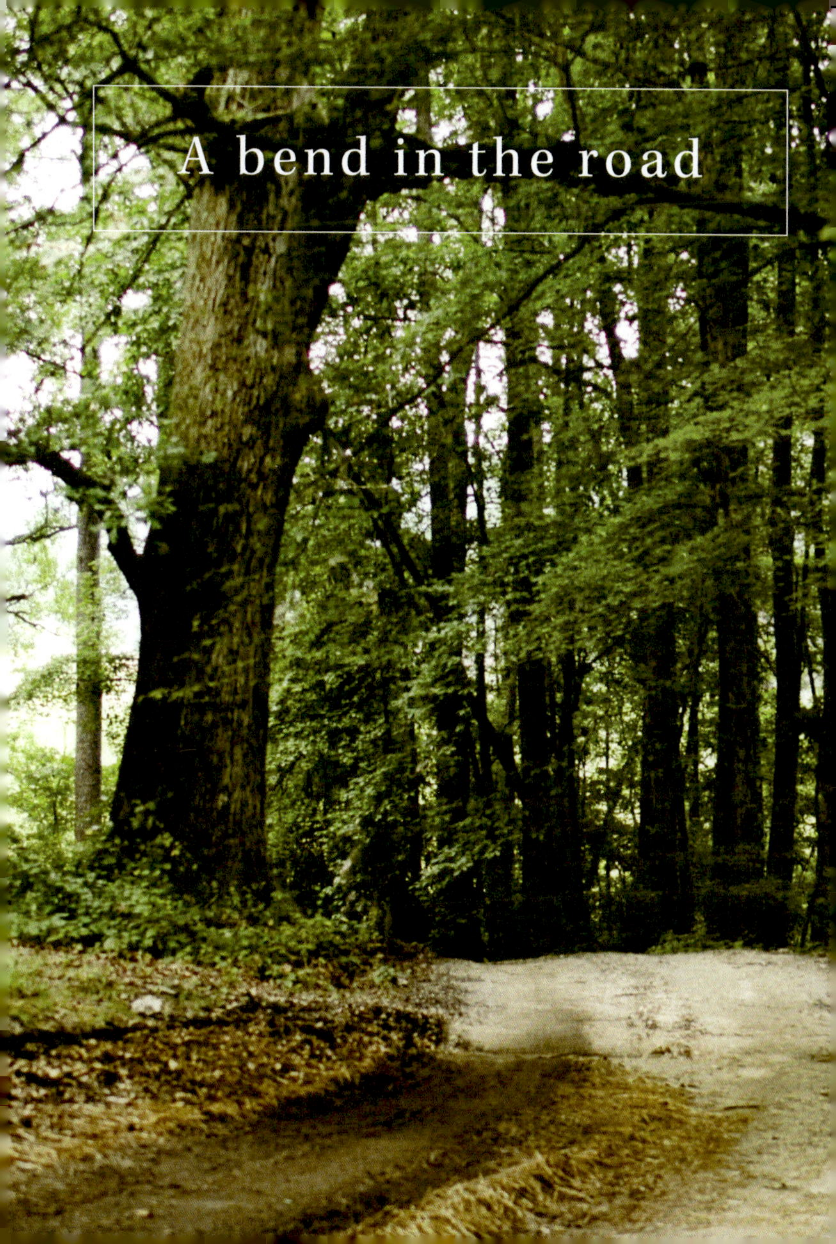

"

It felt as if I had rounded an

unexpected bend in the road and

found a hand to help me along the path.

Leticia's hand. God's hand.

"

SIX

From:	**Brian Saunders**
To:	**Ivan Wild, Craig Bowler**
Date:	**April 28, 2010, 5:47 AM**
Re:	**Moving**

So, I'm being transferred to the Army's College for Officer Training in California. [Salvation Army officers are often given "farewell orders" to move to a new place.] I've spent most of the night mulling this over, working through my feelings. Time to write them out to clear my head ...

Externally, my response is acceptance. I would guess that this has probably been in the works for some time—after all, our average stay anywhere is only three years, and by that meter, our time was up. It's my understanding that the plan had already been in place prior to Leticia's illness. Crestmont [the college] is a good place for us to go. I have little professional interest in it at present, but it is an emotionally good choice;

it is familiar ground, and it would be far harder for us to go somewhere unfamiliar. I also have a deep trust in God—I know that He will give both Holden and me strength to deal with our grief, despite the undeniably more difficult circumstance of moving at this point in our lives. I am sure that although this will undoubtedly hinder our recovery, we will still eventually be OK. God promises to work all things for the good of those who love him, even if He does not promise it will be easy. I can still hear Leticia's words at her last public address, telling the officers of the territory that while the Army makes assignments, appointments come from God; the Army decides where you live, but you decide how you will serve.

No doubt it will be hard to leave. Why would anyone want to? The people here are fantastic and the culture is great. The corps is thriving, and I feel like I have caught my stride. And I'm not sure how I will ever get used to wearing a tie every day again!

I have often preached that life is 10% circumstances and 90% response. It's not what happens to you that matters, but how you deal with it. I recall the lines of that song: "I will go without a murmur/And His footsteps follow still." That's what I am counting on.

Thanks for listening. I needed to get that off my chest.

Brian

From: Ivan Wild

To: Brian Saunders, Craig Bowler

Date: April 28, 2010, 7:25 AM

Re: Re: Moving

I can sense the tension that this brings your way. I feel a bit of the pain here. I am sorry about the struggle you face. I wish it wasn't the case.

Man, I'm trusting God for your response. I'm trusting Him for a "just one more" approach to this possible change. You are right; God will supply what you need, whether it's in Hawaii or at Crestmont. Who knows what God will do. He's a good God and He can be trusted. We know that.

Remember that the Army is not a person; it's an organization. Faith in an organization will ebb and flow. Thankfully we've put our lives in the hands of a Person. Someone we can have a relationship with. Someone who can lead us through the challenges that the organization, or even other people, present to us. As you said, response to the situation is the key.

I'll continue to pray for this whole thing, and pray for God to continue to extend His peace and presence to your heart, and to Holden's. Know He loves you and He will lead you through this.

Ivan

From: Brian Saunders

To: Ivan Wild, Craig Bowler

Date: May 1, 2010; 6:25 AM

Re: Re: Moving

Thanks for that reminder, Ivan. I get it. I'm also trying to figure this grief thing out. It's almost like I have two separate griefs within me competing with each other for attention and priority. Leticia's loss is still raw and harsh, but now I also have a real sense of loss for our lives here in Honolulu. I get that the Army has to move me from time to time. I'm just struggling with "Why now?" when everything seems to be going well at the corps, and when Holden and I least need this disruption in our lives. Surely there are others who could have done the job they want me to do. We've moved lots of times, and usually I'm fine with it. It's just harder this time. It's dealing with these simultaneous griefs—for both Leticia and Hawaii. And then there is guilt. Leticia had often said that Holden's welfare was to be our top priority regardless of ministry responsibilities. Her one worry was that her death would hurt his faith. My current concern is that, in allowing the Army to move me, have I let him down? Have I let her down? Am I being disloyal, or dishonoring her wishes, or hurting Holden? It feels like I have fallen short of my duty to protect him. Yet I find reassurance in the knowledge that God already knows all of this. And that He will make it right. He has a reason for us to go to the mainland. So I'll trust. I'll go. …
All for now.

B.

The most difficult part, of course, was telling Holden. At 14, he was just beginning to create his own identity. He was heavily involved at school and church and with friends. No 14–year–old wants to move away. But his challenge was much greater. He had just lost his mother. His life was already turned upside down. He also knew the Army's system. He knew that they didn't really have to move me—it was just their best option, just part of the plan. He also knew that the Army considers many factors in the transfer system. For instance, they try not to move people when their kids are in high school, or if they have special needs.

Well, as Holden said, who, in the entire Salvation Army has a more pressing need to stay put than us? I understood and agreed with Holden's frustrations entirely. He even called Territorial Headquarters in California to talk to the Secretary for Personnel (the human resources director). I will be forever grateful to Colonel Dave Hudson for taking that call. He listened to Holden with respect and courtesy, taking the time to listen to this teenager vent.

Any list of top stressors for kids shows that the death of a parent is #1, and moving also ranks in the top 10. So Holden was enduring two of the most difficult situations a child can experience at the same time. Hawaii had become home; his friends had become his ohana. These friends had supported him through Mom's illness and death. He was on the school's robotics team and was in position to become the captain. The corps, the Hawaiian culture, and the people were all his home and his comfort zone. Even the house itself was important; it was the place where the physical memories of Mom remained—her decorations on the wall, the furniture where she had set it, the bed she slept in, and the couch we cuddled on together. For both of us, this would be the most difficult move of our lives.

I shared his double sorrow. I was afraid to leave this cocoon of support and security. I was concerned about leaving the physical connection of the home we had shared. How to leave the ohana, the ministry, the culture, and the people we had fallen in love with and who had supported us during the most difficult year of our lives. How to leave behind so much that was Leticia, so much that reminded us of her. How to find confidence in a future that would be completely different—with almost nothing to tie back to Leticia's memory and legacy. I was worried about the radical changes we would have to face—right when we needed routine and security. I was not convinced of the Army's wisdom or rationale for this transfer. Still, I knew we had to accept it and prepare to move.

Needless to say, it was a very difficult month. We dealt with this double grief as best we could—venting to friends to be sure, but focusing on immersing ourselves in our friendships, the culture, and local activities. It was as if we were trying to build up memories that would need to last a long time. The two griefs dueled within me—I was sometimes not sure which one was feeding the other. I was used to being transferred, so moving was not so difficult, but moving away from Leticia's last home was very hard.

From: **Brian Saunders**
To: **Undisclosed Recipients**
Date: **June 14, 2010, 11:39 PM**
Re: **Thoughts at 6 months …**

Dear Family and Friends,

So, as of 3:40 p.m. today, it has been six months since Leticia went Home. (I think that is really the best description—the Bible tells us our citizenship is in Heaven, and of all people, Leticia really got that.)

A weekend of milestones and memories:

A year ago on Saturday Leticia addressed the gathering at the Territorial Officers Councils at Commissioning [the occasion when cadets are ordained and receive their first appointments as officers]. … I still get comments on the power of Leticia's speech. She reminded the officers that it's "OK not to be OK." We don't have to be perfect; we don't even have to be well, as long as we are following God's will. She also commented that although The Salvation Army makes appointments, only God truly sends us. It's not so much the old cliché—"The Army can't send me where God cannot use me." It's more like, "God's reasons for your being there are deeper than anything the Army could have known or planned." Something that so many of us can relate to. Something that I am clinging to as I prepare to leave Honolulu.

That was her last major public engagement—a fitting final address. She did not feel well enough to go to the evening service that night or to the ordination and appointment services the next day. She did—using a cane to stay standing—speak at the corps the following week on Father's Day, but she never spoke in public again, and, after Commissioning, she never felt fully well again.

Sunday was Holden's birthday. They did it up big at the corps, so it was good memories, but of course, it was a bit bittersweet, as all the "firsts" will be. This was his first birthday without his mom. We had a great overnight party at the corps with the teen boys. (Note to self: pick up the Nerf gun bullets before the Sunday worship service.) Of course he had a great time with his friends. He will miss them.

Since today, the 14th, falls on a Monday, the day—sequence leading up to today was identical to that of December. I was following the memories as they played out chronologically—Friday night, when Leticia told me she had met with God and that it was time to let her go; Saturday morning, when I told Holden and we went to talk to her for the last time; then through Sunday and Monday as we held our vigil by her bedside.

Today I picked Holden up from school. We started for home at 3:40 p.m., and we both realized that it was exactly six months to the minute since Mom died. Big moment.

I'm not sure if it feels like a long or a short time. Sometimes it feels like she is so close, as if she will walk through the door any minute. Or I will wake up from this dream as soon as the sun rises. Other times it feels like another life—like she is really gone. It is hard to picture the long—term. I can get through each day—

just get up, get going, do what has to be done. Keep breathing. I can even find purpose and joy in life and ministry. But the future is hard to see or even imagine.

In a couple of weeks Holden and I will leave Oahu. This island has become home in so many ways. I am experiencing what I call "dueling griefs." I continue to grieve over the loss of Leticia; now I grieve over the loss of this adopted home. The emotional ties are obvious: this is where Holden became a teenager, where we found a wonderful ministry and ohana. Where the three of us spent our last minutes as a family. Where Leticia experienced her last moments on Earth. It's hard to leave. But I know God goes with us—and will be with us in Los Angeles. So we go.

Things will change dramatically in the months ahead. Holden will start in a new school and get involved in a new corps. We will arrive at a new home that will not reflect Leticia's style or contain the memories of her presence. Our lives will begin to be filled with people who did not know Leticia. Still, we go with confidence, knowing God goes before us, and that, as Leticia herself said, God has a deeper reason for this change than a simple Salvation Army appointment. It's not about where the Army moves us; it's where God wants us that matters.

Blessings

Brian

From:	Ivan Wild
To:	Brian Saunders, Craig Bowler
Date:	June 16, 2010, 3:08 PM
Re:	Re: Thoughts at 6 months...

Brian:

Powerful words and thoughts. I am glad you are writing them to us. I can't begin to understand but do appreciate your "dueling grief."

I could say the obvious cliché, "everything will work out," but the reality is I don't know how it will work out or how it will go for Holden. But I am glad you are honest; maybe you will never understand the move to Crestmont. I think it is healthy to be able to express yourself to God, your friends, your family, and the Army. It's also good for Holden. He sees it is OK and healing to grieve, to ask questions and not have all the answers.

You are exactly who Holden needs. The love between you guys is evident. You are keeping the charge Leticia gave you and (if the saints do this in Heaven), she is looking down at you and is proud. (I am not sure about the theology.) I say that because while I was at the hospital, there was a moment that I was with Leticia while you were with Holden outside. She was telling me about some of the pictures you had hung. She mentioned that Holden was a special son and you were a special husband ... I saw the look in her face—total peace, total assurance, that Holden was going to be all right because he had you and that's what mattered most ... maybe it's not the place but the position you have with Holden. It's not going to be easy, but the bond between you and Holden is special. Just my thoughts. I wish you were able to stay in Hawaii—free lodging and airport runs for us—but I am glad you will be close. We can meet more often—In−N−Out, Disneyland, and even coffee are more fun with friends.

God Bless,

Ivan

From:	**Brian Saunders**
To:	**Ivan Wild, Craig Bowler**
Date:	**June 17, 2010, 1:23 PM**
Re:	**Re: Re: Thoughts at 6 months...**

Thanks Ivan, I had not heard that story before—means a lot. So the top layer of all that grief, of course, is the most basic—grief over losing Leticia. Hard to explain. Still very real and very present. Leticia is still my first thought of the day and my last at night. Everything that happens I see through the lens of the loss. When something good happens, the first thought is, "I wish Leticia were here to see it." When something goes wrong, I immediately want to tell her. Every decision is prefaced with the inclination to ask her what she thinks. The big issue, of course, is that there's no one right beside me to talk with, to share thoughts and concerns and little comments. I don't want to give the impression that I'm sinking into an abyss. I'm really only like this with you. Thanks for taking all the emotional ups and downs—probably saves other people from having to endure them. And, here's something else: I've really appreciated Arwyn and Craig, the youth leaders at the corps. Since they are around me all day, it's they who have who have to put up with spontaneous, sentimental comments all the time. Good people.

Besides, there's lots of good stuff going on. In some perverse way, I think I've found my stride in ministry here. I'm enjoying the corps, even the part of the ministry that I had usually left to Leticia—building relationships, discipling people. Even before she got sick, I think she and I were both really getting comfortable with the ministry at Kaulu-wela. I feel like I have found "my" preaching style and have finally figured out that elusive balance between business and program, administration and pastoring. When Leticia was alive, we pretty much divided the work according to our strengths—I was the administrator and she was the pastor. She planned; I implemented. I used diplomacy; she used discernment. I taught; she discipled. Now, I am learning the true meaning of holistic ministry by embracing all aspects of our responsibilities as officers and pastors.

She would be very proud of what is happening at the corps. Things are really booming. It really feels like ministry is gelling. She'd also be very proud of Holden. He played first cornet in school band and had an excellent final concert. The entire youth group came; he was the only kid with his own (loud) cheering section. His robotics team went to the

World Championships. Very cool! And he is maturing—spiritually, emotionally and physically. His birthday party was epic. We've had some good times in recent months, and I think that's important for me to remember. Good stuff still happens.

Here's a thought: Father's Day has come and gone. Another "first." My first Father's Day was spent at the neo—natal intensive care unit at Torrance Memorial Hospital. This Father's Day was the first without Leticia. The day will never be the same. True. But I'm still a dad. Something I thank God for every day.

So the movers have come and gone. The painters are here—it will take most of two weeks, so I won't have much time to clean the house. Today is a beach day with the kids. Tomorrow music camp starts. We have 25 kids going. Arwyn and Craig have done a great job with our kids! All being well, the house will be completed, and Holden and I will stay out at camp for the last couple of days and spend time at the beach. Shark diving!

OK, gotta go. thanks again.

Brian

From: Craig Bowler
To: Brian Saunders, Ivan Wild,
Date: June 18, 2010, 4:34 AM
Re: Re: Re: Re: Thoughts at 6 months...

Hey Guys,

Thanks for the notes here. I appreciate both. I also enjoyed talking with both of you guys yesterday. It's always good for my soul.

Brian, I continue to pray for you and this "dueling grief." I pray for trust and confidence in your move to L.A. I see it as a faithful servant doing his best to raise his son and serve his God. I agree with Ivan. You are setting an example of how to follow Jesus no matter the cost. Ultimately, through both griefs, your focus has been on Christ, and could there be a better lesson to teach your kid than that?

This journey is long, and I agree it will not end—at least not here. I praise God for the people who support you and encourage you—they are like lanterns along this dark path—but I also thank Him for His Spirit that continues to minister to you, in you, and through you. Your journey has been such an encouragement to my family and me. I'm a recipient of God's grace being expressed through you in the midst of the journey.

God is in this somewhere. He is more in this stuff than we know. He must be.

I continue to pray that God will lead you. Lately, I've been praying for joy. While I believe there will always be sadness, I know God brings joy. I believe there will always be tenderness and lots and lots of grief, but I continue to pray for healing that will lead you to joy. I recognize that this healing process will only end in eternity, but I pray for a joy that runs deeper than the pain. I was just reading "In this world you will have trouble...." [John 16:33] You know that trouble better than anyone I know, but I thank God for His Spirit that brings us peace and joy.

Love you guys!

cb

Rounding a bend...

So we packed up and moved to California. Suddenly, everything was new: new city, new house, new job, new school, new corps, new friends and colleagues. Almost no aspect of our lives remained as it had been. The exception, of course, was that Holden and I still had each other. We continued to do as much together as possible. We went on a summer vacation and set up our house as a team. We quickly got involved in school and church activities, becoming very busy and keeping our minds and hearts occupied. We decorated the house with a Hawaiian theme, using the same decorations and pictures we had had in the house in Honolulu. We got Disneyland passes and basically tried to set ourselves up in yet another "new normal."

One of my biggest fears in leaving Honolulu was that sense that I would be leaving Leticia behind—that leaving the physical reminders of her would somehow make her memory fade, that physical distance would become emotional distance. But God gave me two gifts after we arrived in California.

Leticia and I had been posted at the College for Officer Training twice before—the last time being just seven years ago. Each officers' quarters (home) is equipped with a "Dispo" (Disposition of Forces)—a Salvation Army phone book of sorts. The binder is permanent and kept in the house; the officer inserts revised pages each year when new appointments are announced. A couple of days after our arrival, I flipped through the pages of the Dispo I found in a kitchen cupboard. There, on a page just inside the back cover, was a note in Leticia's handwriting. She must have written it to me on the sly on an evening when we had guests over: "I need to have a wee bit of dinner, but after we should take everyone to Coldstone."

That's it. It was just a comment—nothing important or sentimental. But as I stood there in the kitchen on that July afternoon I was dumbfounded. How did this single insert page survive seven years of revisions? It must have been in our house when we had lived at Crestmont previously—but that was in a different quarters. How did it migrate here? And why had the page not been thrown away sometime during those seven years? Then, after a moment, the answer became clear—because God wanted me to see it. It was here because God knew I needed to see it. To touch it. Here is her handwriting. Her hand touched this piece of paper. Nothing special—just a slice of ordinary life. But it is a picture of her. Here, in this new house. She's here, in my new life. That page is here on the table as I type these words. A God thing to be sure.

Then, one afternoon during late summer, before all the cadets arrived, I took a stroll around the campus. I was the only one around. I wandered through the faculty quarters, the dining room, the chapel, and the classrooms. A dawning sense of understanding began to ease into my thinking—Leticia had been here too.

We had spent 10 years of our lives together here on this campus—two as cadets and eight as faculty members. It was here that we met and fell in love. It was here that we made our first home together and that our son was born. I was beginning to see her; memories came flooding back. I walked through our old apartment. Our first home. There is where our couch was—right here was our bed.

I walked over to the dining room where we ate lunches together—there was our old table.

The classrooms. This is where she taught; she stood right about there.

I went into the chapel, where Holden was dedicated as a baby and where he was enrolled as a junior soldier. I saw our session flag: "Servants of Jesus," the same flag under which we signed our covenants.* The same flag that stood at our wedding. The same flag that stood over her ashes at her funeral. Here's where we used to sit, and yes, here, at the altar—on the left nearest the side door—was where we prayed together.

*In The Salvation Army, each new class of cadets around the world share a "session name" chosen by International Headquarters. At each training school, the session has its own Salvation Army flag with the session name emblazoned on it. Cadets sign a personal covenant at the time when they are commissioned as officers and ordained as ministers of the Gospel.

Suddenly, I realized that I had not left Leticia in Honolulu at all. It was such a magnificent discovery that I could not believe I had not understood it before. I am convinced that this little afternoon trip down memory lane was part of my journey, a gift from God to assure me of His presence along this path through the valley. It felt as if I had rounded an unexpected bend in the road and found a hand to help me along the path. Leticia's hand. God's hand.

Nov. 25, 2010

Hey babe. Well, it's Thanksgiving. We are here at [brother] Dave & Jennifer's house. Roy and Paula Wild and their kids are here too. Mom and Father and the Gildens are also coming over. It's very different than the Thanksgiving 2010 I had assumed would transpire a year ago today. Virtually everything is different than I had wanted.

So, a year since last Thanksgiving. I guess that's obvious. As we get closer to the anniversary of your going Home, and as these holidays come, I'm thinking of you more and more. Still can't wrap my head around the fact that you really are gone. That you are not coming back. They say holidays and special days are the hardest. I'm not so sure. I think every day is hard. Still, there's probably a reason I'm up here alone in my room on Thanksgiving Day while everyone else is downstairs together.

A year ago today you were in ICU South at Straub Hospital in Honolulu. It had been an up and down week. You had already been in the hospital for over three months. Every time they thought they had your infections beat, something new cropped up. They gave me "the speech" again. I had gotten several of them over the months, but this one was different. Your lows were getting lower, and your highs were not quite so high. So the doctor told me to expect the worst. That you had so many things cascading that it did not look like you would make it. I did not really believe him. Of course, you always say that I am overly optimistic, that I never understand the seriousness of stuff. Perhaps I just did not want to believe. I remember sitting alone in your room; you were in deep sleep, unconscious. I prayed so deeply, pleading with God not to take you, pleading with you not to go. It started to sink in that maybe this was real. I went home that night after kettles with a greater burden than I had felt since you entered the hospital.

Yet Holden and Mom had made dinner for you, and I really wanted us to have Thanksgiving together. The Army's big Thanksgiving dinner was being held at the Blaisdale Center just across the street from the hospital. I was determined to do my duty over there, then come back to you. So I juggled the day. Started it at the hospital. I walked in, and there you were, sitting up, wide awake, watching TV. I think I almost cried. You had been asleep for four full days. Now you were up! I really do believe that God granted us a special miracle that day. You were weak but awake and alert. We talked about mundane stuff a bit and then you had some tests to do, so I went over to Blaisdale to play with the band. Holden and my Father were there. I did my bit and headed back to the hospital. Hung out for a while, but you were asleep. Went back to Blaisdale and helped clean up. I felt pretty good that I could do both—spend time with you and still complete my responsibilities. Of course, no one really expected me to do much; I didn't even have an assignment. But still, you know me, always wanting the best of both worlds, trying to be everything to everyone. I try not to think in terms of "would have, should have," but obviously I should have abandoned all pretense of working and spent every hour with you. But I honestly thought you'd be coming home soon, so I thought I was doing the right thing.

I remember telling Dusty and Randy and Jeff and Elosia

that you were up and alert, and that God had granted us a Thanksgiving miracle; that even though you still had some serious stuff to deal with, you were OK for today, and that was enough for now. Holden and my parents went home and we had our own little Thanksgiving dinner. All the normal stuff. You would have liked it, although I must say that Mom's stuffing is not as good as yours.

Stuffing—now there is one of those very pragmatic things. Why is that such a big deal? I really liked your stuffing, and knowing that I will never have it again is really hard for some reason. It shouldn't be a big deal, and in the whole scheme of things of course it is not, but I still really grieve over it. Weird.

After we ate, Holden and I went back to the hospital to bring you your dinner. We had it all packed in little Tupperware containers. Gluten−free and ready to eat. When we got there you were reading a magazine but complained that they kept moving your stuff away from you. A good sign to me—you had the energy to complain! So you ate your dinner, and we sat around. I told you all about Blaisdale and kettles, but I did not tell you about Dr. Doom. Suddenly, his predictions seemed unwarranted yet again. Eventually, you got tired, and it was time to let you sleep. So we did our usual custom of taking notes on what you wanted brought to the hospital and getting you all arranged for the night, with stuff you needed close at hand, all tucked in under your pink and green blanket. A prayer and a kiss, and we went home. Our last Thanksgiving.

I wonder how much you remember? How much of the time in the hospital were you awake and cognizant? For most of the hospitalization, you were fully aware and awake. Directing staff, teaching the student nurses, reading, watching TV, etc. But were there times when you were so weak and drowsy that you didn't remember the day before? Toward the end, I think you were more tired. Most of our conversations were very mundane anyway. Since I really believed you'd get better, I never thought we needed to have deeper conversations—besides, that would just scare both of us.

But what about now? I wonder how much you remember now? What memories come with us to Heaven? If there is no sorrow, are there no painful memories? Do you remember the hospital in those last weeks? Are you now aware of how I sat at your bedside, crying, holding your hand, and asking you to stay? I assume we retain our personal selves; who we are as humans is essentially who we are as eternal souls. But what are we conscious of? Do you know what is going on here, on Earth, in human time? Are you aware of the passage of what we call time? Or does it all happen instantaneously; we all arrive together with no consciousness of the passage of time since our own deaths? Will we share memories? Once I arrive, will I "catch you up" on everything that has happened? Will we care? ...

So, here we are. Holden and I are at Dave & Jennifer's house. It was a good day. Kids played football all morning and had Nerf gun battles all afternoon. We played our usual game of "Acquire." No one really mentioned you, but I've been thinking about you all day long. I guess it's just part of the grieving process; the holidays and anniversaries of events intensify the grief. And the day unfolds around me. No one knows the battles going on in my head—fighting over wanting to share in the fun, be happy and jovial, yet at the same time wanting to sit alone and remember our Thanksgivings together. Interesting the way the brain works, and the stuff that suddenly becomes important. I wish I had taken a picture while you were in the hospital. I wish I had learned your stuffing recipe. I wish I could have had one more Thanksgiving with you.

Mile markers

"

Milestones provide perspective
and point the way both forward
and backward.

"

SEVEN

From: **Brian Saunders**
To: **Undisclosed Recipients**
Date: **December 14, 2010, 08:19 AM**
Re: **ONE YEAR AGO**

Dear Friends,

Today marks one year since Leticia went Home. I'm not sure how one is supposed to mark the day, but for me at least, I think writing may be an appropriate recognition. It's certainly therapeutic for me.

So, here's the update on Leticia. As I said at her funeral, quoting one of her favorite hymns, "It is well with [her] soul." She is doing well. In fact, she's more well than we can possibly imagine. It would not surprise you to know that the theology of eternity has become very real and personal to me in recent months. Those of you who have lost loved ones will certainly understand. Suddenly all those clichés about people "waiting for us" become concrete. Vague ideas about being in the Presence of God, of walking the golden streets and entering the Pearly Gates become solid images in our minds. Whatever the timeline is—if such terminology is even meaningful—I can definitely picture Leticia enjoying her new Home.

I wrote some months ago about one of my favorite memories of Leticia being one where she is singing a praise and worship chorus at church. She always loved singing, especially songs about Heaven and eternity. This particular occasion was a Sunday not long before she went into the hospital. We were standing in the front row in the chapel at Kauluwela in Honolulu. Her eyes were closed, her head tilted up, a smile radiant upon her face. The song was "I'm trading my sickness / I'm trading my pain / I'm laying it down for the joy of the Lord." It was always one of her favorites.

Now here's the interesting part. That memory has now morphed into a recurring dream. The image is of Leticia—same song, same expression, but the location has changed. I see her now among the throng at the base of a great gold and white throne. Face lifted up toward the throne far above her. Eyes closed. Praising God in pure joy and contentment. She has indeed traded the sickness and sorrow of this world. Not that sickness defined her in this world—it did not—but she certainly traded in those last months of sickness for an eternity of joy. And while I might selfishly wish she were still next to me singing that song, deep down I know that I am glad she is there, getting to fulfill the desires of her heart. The reality is that, now that she has experienced Heaven, I would not want her to have to return to Earth. Such a desire seems somehow selfish. She is where she belongs. Certainly I am still grieving, but the grief has also turned to real happiness. A deep, abiding joy that she is exactly where she always wanted to be. Exactly where God wants her to be.

That brings me to another thought I've had of late. Something new and surprising has surfaced: I have always felt pride in having been associated with Leticia. Pride in her accomplishments and her ministry, pride in the way she raised our son, pride in her creativity, honesty, integrity, and strength. But now, seemingly unannounced and unbidden, a new kind of pride has begun surfacing, a pride not just in having known the earthly Leticia, but in knowing the heavenly Leticia—the one who is in the presence of Almighty God. As strange as this sounds, I am proud that I know Leticia now, in her current, eternal life. Imagine the enormity of the thought and the theology behind it: I know someone who is the presence of God Himself. It's like I have an "in" in Heaven. It's like saying, "Hey, I know someone on the inside." Naturally, I know others who have gone to be with the Lord, but there is something different, something special, something ever so personal about my Leticia being in Heaven. Someone that I have known so well, so intimately, is now with God. It's like I have a whole new connection to God. So there is pride, but it is also ever so humbling. Wow, Leticia, my Leticia, is with the Creator!

One more thought rattling around in my brain: While I have come to accept that Leticia is no longer here with us in body, that does not mean that she is not still a part of our family. This is so comforting. It's not that our little family has been reduced from three to two; it's just that our arrangement has changed. It is still Leticia, Holden, and I. Holden and I here, Leticia in Heaven. Holden and I will (probably) grow old, and things will forever be different, but no matter what, Leticia will still be included in our family. She is very much a part of who we are; anyone who knows of Holden's stubborn streak will agree! So our family is no longer together, but it is still our family.

Speaking of family, I should also give a report on Holden and me. In a nutshell, we are OK. We take it one day at a time. Our lives are very different now than they were a year ago. New home, new school, new job. And of course, adapting to life without Leticia. Nothing is like it was a year ago yesterday. I'm so very grateful for the support of so many friends and family members who have come alongside us over these past 12 months. Not sure what state we would be in without your prayers and support. Holden is very busy with school, extracurricular activities (marching band, robotics), church (brass band, songsters [choir] and other activities). He's on track to get his pilot's license soon. And of course I am busy with my responsibilities at the training college. Being busy is good for us. We continue to enjoy cooking together, and Holden has become quite accomplished in the kitchen. All in all, we are learning, growing, and moving forward.

So it's been a year. At six months, I noted that I was not sure if it had felt like a long time or a short time. Now I can say that it's very hard to believe an entire year has gone by. A year ago today Holden and I arrived at the hospital early in the morning after a very short night at home, knowing that this would probably be the day. She had last spoken 48 hours before. We set our chairs, had a prayer, and waited. A strangely peaceful day. At 3:40, Hawaii time, she quietly went Home. Tonight, as 6:40 PST approaches, Holden and I will be at home, surrounded by some very good friends. I'm not sure how to commemorate this milestone, but I am deeply appreciative of their presence.

A wise and dear friend (thanks, Stan!) recently sent me a link to a video. It's a boy's choir. As Stan so aptly said, perhaps this is what Leticia was singing during her last moments with Holden and me on Earth. ... Perhaps this is what angels sound like ...

Shadows gone, break of day / Real life has begun / I'm just going home.

Brian

Milestones provide perspective and point the way both forward and backward. We celebrate holidays and accomplishments and note the passage of time with anniversaries and ceremonies. We mark our lives by events and accomplishments—birthdays, graduations, weddings, and funerals. They are signposts along the way.

December 25, 2010, 7:15 AM

Dear Leticia,

It's Christmas Day. I know it's a bit weird to write to you, but I have found it helpful to write—I've written to other people; I've written to myself; and so, as I did at Thanksgiving, I decided to write to you again for Christmas.

We are at David and Jennifer's house. Joshua is 9, Matthew is 7, and Emily is 5. Perfect ages for Christmas. Holden is 15, but he still really enjoys playing with his cousins, and is a pretty good "big brother."

Holden's last day of school was Friday. We went to dinner and a movie with the Brackenburys that night. On Saturday Holden and I went to Target and the mall (yeah, on the Saturday before Christmas, crazy, I know!) to do all our Christmas shopping. Holden was quite pleased since this is the first time he's had both a job and a debit card, so he could shop for my gifts by himself. It was strange not to be buying gifts for you. I kept seeing stuff and thinking, "Leticia would love this." Interesting that my thought process has moved from "Leticia *will* like this ... " to Leticia *would* like this." I guess the acceptance stage is moving in. Still, I have to tell you that it still feels surreal. As if my entire life is just a dream that I will eventually wake up from, to find you lying in bed next to me. Or more like we are just going through the motions, waiting for you to return so we can pick up where we left off and get life back to normal. I keep thinking there is so much we have to tell you to get you caught up. Maybe that's why these writings are so important and therapeutic for me—it's a way of expressing these feelings and recording the events of our lives since I don't have anyone to tell anymore.

So back to the story. We actually wrapped all the presents on Saturday night, so we were basically ready for Christmas a week early. The next day we drove to Sacramento to spend Christmas week with the family.

Friday was Christmas Eve. A slow start in the morning, another football game, then we made gingerbread houses. You'd be impressed; like you did once, we used graham crackers instead of gingerbread. Holden actually made a good–looking one. Surprising, I know, since he does not have a creative bone in his body! You would have been pleased.

After decorating the houses, we went to church for the family Christmas Eve service. Then to my parents' house for dinner and to open Christmas stockings they had made for us and our traditional gift, pajamas. Finally, home, where the kids got ready and into bed. We stayed up for a little while watching "A Christmas Story"—yeah, your favorite—then Dave & Jen put out the rest of the presents and we all went to bed.

This morning I woke up very early—could not stay asleep. Joshua was awake around 6, so I went in and we talked; he was not supposed to get out of bed until 7, then could not go downstairs until 7:30. Holden got up around 7, so they played video games until everyone else woke up.

We started with the stockings, had breakfast, then, once the grandparents arrived at 9:30, we started on presents. I've never been with a larger family before, so it was a bit different. They do presents the same way we do—one at a time. So it took until past noon. Dinner was at 2—a sirloin roast with parmesan mashed potatoes. After cleanup, dessert was a triple chocolate cake. Jennifer is an excellent cook. Naturally, it makes me miss your cooking.

Technically this is our second Christmas without you. But it really feels as if it is the first. Last Christmas was sandwiched between your two funerals, and it felt as if you were just still in the hospital. In fact, since we were so used to you being in the hospital, it just felt normal—like we were heading off to see you after lunch ... Obviously, I was still in the classic "denial" phase. This year, everything is different: the pace, the people, the traditions. I guess that's good in a way, since not much reminds me of you. Your name comes up—which I always appreciate but because we are not in our house, or doing "our" traditions, it does not pull on the heartstrings as much. Although I did get a bit misty-eyed during "Silent Night" at the church service last night. It reminded me forcefully of two years ago, when we watched Holden in the live Nativity at DHQ (divisional headquarters) in Manoa. Remember that? It was the night before Christmas Eve. I let the team deal with the kettles that night so I could take some time off. We dropped off my parents and Holden so they could get ready, and then we returned for the show. We parked and walked down the walkway. You took my hand. We sat on the wall and watched the show. For a few minutes, I forgot all about kettles, Angel Tree, corps programs, and everything else. We just got to watch this wonderful depiction of the Nativity, beautiful music and all, with our son participating. Too soon it was over. A cherished memory. Why does the simple act of holding hands bring such positive feelings? It was the whole thing, wasn't it? Christmas, Holden, music, lights—it was all perfect. And we were together with no thought to responsibilities and duties. Nice.

So this is our second Christmas without you. It's different. We've not had Christmas in someone else's house since before Holden was born. Even so, it's been a very nice day. You would be proud of Holden. He handled today very well indeed.

I miss you—and days like today are especially difficult. But I also know that you are OK. And so are we. Just not quite so OK as if you were here.

One of the most difficult moments for me was the realization that we would never have a "normal" Christmas again. It goes back to all those little traditions and ways of doing things that make the holidays special: the decorations, the food, the passing out of gifts, the simple comfort of being home, relaxing, enjoying each other's company. Each family has its own way of doing this, its own little traditions.

Here's something very specific: I miss Leticia's cinnamon rolls, which we had every Christmas morning. I have no idea which recipe she used, so I can't recreate it. It's all gone now, and it will never come back. And we will probably never spend another Christmas at home. Now, that does not mean that the holidays are not enjoyable. They can still be special and memorable. But now Christmas will always be at someone else's house, with their traditions and ways of doing things. It's nice, just not quite the same.

At Dave and Jen's, we made a point of keeping a couple of our personal traditions. The good news is that they completely understood and did their best to make us feel comfortable and at home. One example: We have a certain Christmas music CD we listen to every year. It is the first CD we put in the car on the first day of kettles, and, because it has a lovely rendition of "Silent Night," it's the last song we listen to on Christmas Eve. Last year, returning to Dave and Jen's house after the Christmas Eve service, Holden asked Uncle Dave to play it. The song had not quite ended when we reached the house, so we just sat in the driveway, listening until the final notes faded away. A nice touch.

An unexpectedly difficult decision

Who would have thought shaving could become such an ordeal? I do it every day. It's just part of life. Most of my adult life I've been clean–shaven, which seems to suit me. I tried a mustache for a while but quickly decided it wasn't for me. Then, 10 years ago, I decided to try something new.

We were on vacation, having just been transferred from

England to take up our new assignments at the training college. I hadn't shaved for a week, but vacation was over, and it was time to get out the razor and report for our new responsibilities. I shaved off the sides, but, on impulse, left a goatee in place. I showed Leticia, who immediately liked it. She said it made me look older, more distinguished—a trait she thought would serve me well, as I was younger than many of the cadets I was to teach. The beard had an aura of academia about it, she said. I wasn't so sure, but hey, I figured, my wife likes it, so I'll keep it.

I kept it through that appointment and the next. For 10 years. Every once in a while I'd ask Leticia if I should shave it off. No, she would say, she liked it. Who am I to argue? So it stayed. But I was growing increasingly tired of it. In Guam and Hawaii, the humidity made it itch, and it was a bother to maintain.

Six months after Leticia went Home, when Holden and I moved back to the training college, the goatee seemed like a good idea again. But the more I thought about it, the more I realized I didn't really like it. So I began contemplating shaving it off. Months went by, then an entire year. I thought about it, continued to ponder—why is this so hard?

Normally, this would not be a big deal for me. I'm not all that particular, and I'm not style-conscious. But, as I went to shave it off one day, I couldn't bring myself to do it. I realized that the only reason I had kept it all those years was because Leticia had liked it. I had kept it for her. So now I had a dilemma. Do I keep it or shave it off? Perhaps I should keep it,

I thought; it reminds me of her, and she liked it. Shaving it off seemed disloyal—as if I were setting her wishes aside, letting go of another part of her. On the other hand, it's been a long time. I have to be myself, and to start "moving on." (Man, I hate that phrase!)

All through the summer, I asked people what they thought. With most people, I just asked the superficial question: "What do you think, goatee or no goatee?" Of course, they were no help whatsoever. "Oh, whatever you want, Brian"; "You look fine either way." Yeah, right. I don't need coaching. I need someone to make the choice for me, to take the burden of the decision off me. With some people, I probed deeper: "Is it wrong to shave it off? Am I dishonoring her?" The answer is obvious. Of course not. She would not—and certainly now does not—mind one way or the other. The real question is: Am I ready? I knew I wanted to shave it off—for my own comfort, my own self–image. But I'd already let go of so many connections to Leticia: moving from Hawaii, donating her clothes, packing away her jewelry and belongings. Was I ready to let go of this particular connection?

Yesterday morning I shaved off the goatee. It's the first time I've been clean–shaven for 10 years. Feels a bit strange, a bit naked. But I think I like it. I like the way it looks, and I'm growing comfortable with it. Most important, I feel OK about it. I can do this. I can keep moving forward. Here's the lesson I'm learning: Even the smallest things connect me to Leticia. She is still a part of me, connected to every decision I make. Yet I'm learning to stand on my own two feet. Not fun, but doable. So yeah, I lost the goatee. Who knows, maybe I'll grow it back some day. But for now, I'm OK.

From:	Brian Saunders
To:	Ivan Wild, Craig Bowler
Date:	March 28, 2011, 9:28 AM
Re:	Dream

We are in Hawaii for Craig & Arwyn's wedding. Just woke up from a really tough dream—the whole sweat–pouring, bolting–upright–in–bed kind of wake–up. I'm not really sure I'd call it a nightmare, since I liked it. Very, very vivid dream. I had found a little blue box of silver jewelry with an old letter from Leticia inside. I was just about to open it when Holden came in and needed help finding his uniform for church. When I went back to get the box, it was gone. I ran through the house (our Honolulu house) looking for it, getting more and more anxious. Apparently my parents were visiting. My dad said he had moved it along with a pile of clothes to the back room. I guess it was Holden's room, but all his stuff was gone—looked as if I had already cleaned out the house to move. So I found the box and sat on the floor facing the back wall with my side against the wall. I opened the box and began reading the letter; it was an old love note, something that I had written to Leticia 20 years ago that she had saved in her little silver box. Then a shadow came across my face and an arm reached around me. It was Leticia. She asked, "What are you looking at?" I turned and saw her. She was wearing a blue sweater, with a checked shirt, the same outfit I had seen her wear countless times. I stared at her hard, somehow knowing she was not supposed to be here. Emotions flooded my heart. I was incredulous but relieved; for a second, I thought the last year had all been a dream. Then, suddenly, the truth hit, and I knew it was a dream. Immediately, I woke up. Man, it was hard. But at the same time, it had been really good to see her again. Not sure if that makes sense, but if felt so real, it's as if I actually saw her again.

Anyway, I'm OK, just wanted to record the dream, and figured I'd tell you. I'm sure it has to do with the emotions of being back in Hawaii. Thanks as always for listening.

b.

From: **Brian Saunders**
To: **Ivan Wild, Craig Bowler**
Date: **May 5, 2011, 9:35 PM**
Re: **It happened again**

Holden and I went on his first driving lesson the other day. Today we did another quick drive around campus. As I was considering how cool this was, my thoughts naturally went to "Man, Leticia is gonna be so proud," quickly replaced by, "She *would* be proud if she could see this," then to, "God, I so desperately wish she could see this." Tears welled up and I struggled to hold it together as Holden drove (not the place to distract him!). It hits suddenly like that sometimes—and I need a moment like this to share it. So, there it is. There is such pain in knowing that she is missing so much, that she will never see Holden grow up, and that Holden will never get to share these joys with her. I know the tears will flow when Holden flies solo for the first time. When he graduates. When he gets his pilot's license. They will come again at each milestone. There are now no fully "good" things—even the best are tinged with melancholy. Tears don't scare me, but the pain is so real and visceral. Man, it's hard. I just wish she were here.

No need to call. You know I write these things more for me than for you. I just need to share.

b

From: **Brian Saunders**
To: **Undisclosed Recipients**
Date: **June 14, 2011, 11:31 PM**
Re: **18 Months**

Dear Friends,

just a quick note this evening ...

Today marks 18 months since Leticia went Home. As usual, the 14th of the month is a bit more somber than most days. But it's OK.

It's been a weekend of emotions and milestones. My first Commissioning back on staff at the training college, preparing for a trip to Australia with the Pasadena Tabernacle Songsters, Holden's 16th birthday ... and of course this 18-month milestone. It goes without saying that I wish Leticia could be here to see this weekend. She loved the ministry at the training college. She loved young adults and cadets in particular. We were privileged to be on staff for eight years together, and she was always moved to tears at the covenant and ordination services. The responsibility to train and equip new officers is a sacred mandate. She would have been pleased that I only messed up one name in announcing the cadets as they walked across the platform!

And of course she would have loved to see Holden taking flight lessons. She would have been bursting with pride. This is a dream we had shared as a family. It was one of the last things she promised him—that Dad would do everything in his power to support his dream to become a pilot. He's almost there.

So, the big question people continue to ask me is: "How are you doing these days?" I've come to understand a few things in recent months. I find that it is getting easier to talk about Leticia. I've always enjoyed hearing other people's stories about her—how she influenced them, or taught them something, or just that they appreciated her smile and care. I find that I can share about her as well. That it does not hurt; in fact, it's therapeutic. It's also a part of her legacy; it's my opportunity to share the woman I knew with others who did not have the opportunity to know her.

I've also come to understand the dichotomy of distance. The more time passes, the "easier" my path becomes; but at the same time, the longer I am on this journey, the farther away from Leticia I get. I grow concerned that, with the passing of time, Leticia will become a faded memory, a relic of the past, no longer relevant, no longer known. I suppose that's part of legacy as well.

I also don't want her to become just a perfected memory, a PhotoShopped picture, a distorted caricature of herself. We tend to do that after people die. "Don't speak ill of the dead," we say. A good policy, to be sure, but doesn't that rob the person of their personality, of their true self? None of us is perfect, and although we like to remember the positives, there is benefit from also recalling the whole person. I prefer the real, imperfect Leticia. The one who had faults and failures as well as faith and holiness. I want to display the candid snapshot, not the retouched portrait.

I just completed a paper for a class at Fuller. Because the class was on emotional, spiritual, and physical health, I chose to write on my journey through this grief over the past 18 months. The paper was both therapeutic and emotionally challenging. Early each morning and late into each night for the past several weeks, I have walked myself back through these past months, examining my emotions, my coping mechanisms, and my responses while reliving the deep sorrow and grief. I have come to understand that while there is no end to this dark valley, there are plenty of lamps along the way. Holden and I surrounded by friends and companions who walk beside us, shining their light into our lives. They are friends who care, who ask about us, pray for us, and continue to remind us of Leticia's influence in their lives. They are godly friends who remind us that God himself walks beside us all along the way. So tonight, on this 18–month anniversary of Leticia's passing, I just wanted to say thanks, each of you, for shining your lights along my path. Thank you for your friendship, your prayers, your counsel, your ears, and sometimes, your simple silence. I appreciate you more than I can express. Thanks for walking alongside me.

Blessings

brian

And there are other kinds of milestones as well—special events and activities, accomplishments or achievements that are not connected to holidays. Birthdays, anniversaries, graduations, promotions, awards, vacations, and trips create memories and stir emotions. As we approach the second anniversary of Leticia's death, I can't help but reflect on some of the milestones of the past two years.

During the last 24 months, Holden has been to World Championships with his robotics team from Hawaii and is now co–captain of his team here in Rancho Palos Verdes. We've been to Washington, D.C., taken a Disney Cruise, and been on vacations to the Bahamas and Mexico. We are members of a couple of the Army's premier music groups, and have been on a songster (choir) trip to Australia and New Zealand, and a band trip to New England. Holden has ramped up his flight lessons and will soon have his private pilot's license. We've moved, and I've had two appointments. Last month I let him drive for the first time. All these milestones have passed without Leticia's presence. Every one is tinged with a slight sense of melancholy. We still have a good time, and we still appreciate the significance of the moment; we just have a quiet recognition that Leticia is not here.

There are special days—like our anniversary or Leticia's birthday or my birthday, or Holden's for that matter—that will continue to chafe. Anniversaries of other sorts—like our kidney transplant, first date, or final conversation—will also come and go with added significance. But I choose to mark them not with sorrow but with gratitude. Gratitude for a life given, a joy shared, and a heart blessed by this wonderful woman who was with us for all too short a time.

Ever since the first anniversary of Leticia's death, we have spent that evening—December 14—with friends. It's not meant to be a memorial, just an opportunity to share the evening with loved ones who have been part of the journey.

From: Brian Saunders

To: John Brackenbury, Pam Brackenbury, Cindy
            Dickinson, Mike Dickinson, Jennifer Wild, Ivan Wild

Date: December 15, 2011, 7:51 AM

Hi,

Just a quick note to say thanks for coming last night. It really
meant a lot to me to have you all here. I'm sure you will not
be surprised to know I couldn't sleep last night. I woke up at
about 2:30, fully awake. As I sat there, I pondered the evening, and thought of a couple of things ...

Last year on the same evening we planned to order pizza.
Everyone was sitting around chatting, and I realized that I
had better actually place the order. So, while you were all in
the living room, I crossed over to the kitchen to make the call.
I glanced over at the clock on the oven—6:40 PST exactly.
The moment Leticia died. It was as if God gave me that single
minute alone—nothing more, nothing less. You were all
talking and laughing; it was a light, fun, evening, just as we
had planned. I was suitably distracted until that very moment.
God engineered it so I would have it—just a matter of a dozen
seconds or so—alone. Not long enough to sink into grief, but
long enough to mark the moment, the exact one—year anniversary of Leticia's death.

And last night, something similar happened. We were waiting
for the rice cooker to finish. All the other food was laid out
on the counter, and everyone was hanging out nearby. Mike

and I finally decided to check the rice, found it was done, and announced it was time to eat. I asked Ivan to pray. As he started, I happened to glance at the oven clock again; I was a bit irritated that the rice cooker had taken so long. The clock said exactly 6:40. As Ivan prayed, he did not mention Leticia. He didn't need to. I knew it was another moment from God, a prayer at exactly the moment of her death. I'm sure there is no theological or eternal significance attached; it was just a tiny gift from God. It was just right.

The other thing I thought about was from a little later in the evening, when Pam and Cindy shared that they had, earlier that day, read the paper I had written on grief for my class at Fuller, and it had made them cry. I shrugged it off with a grin, saying I didn't mean to shut down the work of The Salvation Army today. I am sorry that I responded to your feelings so glibly. As I thought about it, I realized why; I am still not good with the emotions of this. That is exactly why I am comfortable writing. I have grown comfortable talking about Leticia, and I've even started to be able to share about her death, but there is still this macho thing about denying emotions—even when they are a reaction to my own emotive writings. Another step in the grieving process, another lesson to learn; I need to grow comfortable with the emotions of others as well as my own. Thanks for being unwitting teachers. As you can guess, writing about it this morning is part of my learning and coping process.

Thanks again. Love you guys.

Brian

To: **Brian Saunders, Ivan Wild**
From: **Craig Bowler**
Date: **December 17, 2011, 4:24 AM**

Thanks for this Brian. I'm glad that you were surrounded by friends and family as you moved through some of the dates of last week. More than that, it's obvious to me how you were surrounded by such a present Heavenly Father who walked with you through the week.

This thing about your emotions—I think that's awesome. Engaging fully in your emotions is another step toward wholeness. I think that's true for any person, in any situation of loss. To not express our emotions is to refuse to allow a part of ourselves to fully live. I think it's important for you to express yourself emotionally. These emails and the paper are ways of doing just that. I'm not sure that expressing emotion requires a flood of tears, or a burst of anger, or a joy that causes hands to be thrown into the air in celebration, but I do think these emails are a great way for you to express yourself emotionally. So, keep them coming.

Love you, man. I'll be praying as you move through these weeks. Pray for me. I need it.

cb

To: **Brian Saunders, Craig Bowler**
From: **Ivan Wild**
Date: **December 17, 2011, 7:48 AM**

Great thoughts. Though I cannot fully understand, you and Holden are always part of our family. Every time I read your stuff, I am moved and praise God for a friend that walks with God. Keep writing. And keep walking through this. —Ivan

If these milestones are like mile markers along the path, then the people in our lives are like lanterns shining in the darkness of the valley. Each one helps to make the way brighter, each step easier, each day less about the past and more about the future. It's all about letting God's love — and the love of others—share in those milestones and memories.

Milestones are opportunities to celebrate, to mark the passage of time, and to acknowledge achievements. But they can be hard.

Today was one such milestone, Holden's first day of his senior year at high school. We have a pretty good routine in the mornings; I get up, shower, and dress, then he gets up while I do my devotions and tackle emails. Usually I make us both a glass of chocolate milk. Holden has a 7:00 a.m. class again this year, so we leave the house by 6:40 every morning. We've been doing this routine for a couple of years now. Today was no different. But I couldn't help but think back four years ago, to his first day of high school. I have a great picture of him in front of our house in Honolulu. He is wearing glasses, hair spiked up, black pants, and black polo—his choice of the school uniform options. I took the picture to show Leticia later that day.

Because she wasn't at home. She was already in the hospital. In fact, she spent the entire first three months of Holden's high school experience in the hospital. The rest of it she has spent in Heaven. So today I took another picture—not for Leticia, but for me. I can't help but think, "Man, how's he's grown." He's a young man now—17. Today is the beginning of the end of his childhood. And the normal emotional tug: "Mom would be so proud." The now–familiar thought: "I wish you were here to see this." It's been a frequent refrain over the past three years. Leticia is missing so much, and I hate that both Holden and I have to experience life without her. It breaks my heart to look at Holden's experiences and accomplishments, knowing he cannot share them with his biggest fan; his greatest coach.

There will be many more milestones this year as he finishes high school: Sometime soon, he'll take his first solo flight. Then his last marching band competition and his final robotics meet. He'll obtain his pilot's license, graduate, turn 18, and head off to college. Five years from now he will graduate from university. He'll probably get married and have kids. All of which Leticia will miss. All of which I'll watch, wishing Leticia could see it—both for Holden's sake and for mine.

I know that by the time we see each other again, all these seemingly marvelous accomplishments and milestones won't mean much, but I can't help thinking about all the things I want to tell her, all the stories and details. I do catch myself sometimes. As I'm doing something special or watching something exciting, or experiencing something new, my subconscious is registering, "I can't want to tell Leticia about this ... Oh, wait. I can't."

The truth is, Leticia is never far from my thoughts. As the months and the years unfold, as milestones come and go, as new experiences and memories build upon the old ones, she is still there, somewhere in the background—apart from, but a part of, everything that I do.

The key to these milestones is to create new memories to add to the old so that our memories of these special days are not all from the ever–dimming past. To recognize that good things can still happen, and that we can still enjoy life. It's not that I want to replace the past, just that I need to add to it so the special days don't become weighted down with sorrow. So, new experiences are good, even while we honor traditions that recapture a bit of the past. Leticia is part of my past; she is also part of my present. Every new milestone, every special event or holiday includes her—even if just in my heart. And life continues. There are new joys to experience, new celebrations to enjoy. So I don't fear milestones or holidays anymore. I celebrate them, enjoying them along with everyone else—knowing that, as long as I am here, so is Leticia.

Lights & shadows

"

Prayer is entering into a Presence
and a peace that passes all understanding.
It brings comfort and balm. But it
does not always bring answers.

"

EIGHT

MY 11TH-GRADE ENGLISH literature teacher once told me, "Avoid clichés like the plague." Good pun—fitting for a lit teacher. I also happen to think he's right, up to a point. Clichés are a necessary evil. They can be inane, trite, often thoughtless, usually careless, but they are meant with genuine care and concern. They speak for us when we don't know what to say. I've heard them all.

Some are focused on Leticia: "She's in a better place." "She's not suffering anymore." "She's at peace." Others are an attempt at theological depth: "God's ways are a mystery." "God's will be done." Or an appeal to her legacy: "Her task on earth was finished." Some are aimed at psychological healing: "She'll live forever in our memories." Some attempt to plumb the depths of God's wisdom: "God's timing is always perfect." Others are just nonsense: "God wanted her closer to Him." The ones that particularly irk me are the ones that try to put a positive spin on things: "God will use this for His Glory." Worse yet: "Your own ministry will be stronger as you go through this tragedy." (Yeah, I almost hit the guy.)

Sure, I have my memories of Leticia, but she will *not* live forever in my mind. Indeed, that is exactly what she won't be doing. Yes, our memories of our departed loved ones—impressions of her ideas and opinions—are in our brains. Our perceptions of her reside in our memories—but those are not actually *her*. Leticia—the actual person, the actual body, mind, ideas, and emotions—is gone.

Sure, God's will is a mystery, and perhaps she was indeed finished with all God wanted her to accomplish on earth, but I don't really have to agree with God here, do I? Accept, yes; agree, not so much.

How could He say her task was done—when Holden was just a teenager, when I still needed her?

Sure, she is in Heaven—a decidedly better place—but what comfort is that to me? I'm here. It's not her that is in pain; it's me. Oh, I know the idea of her being released from earthly suffering is a good thing—and I'm very glad for her—but the selfish part of me still dwells on my loss.

The truth is, though, that I wouldn't want her back. Not now. Not after she has experienced Heaven. Not after she has spent time at Home. How could someone who loved her really want her to have to come back to this world with all its ills and woes and sorrows and sin? How utterly selfish!

Even if it was not for my sake, but for my son's. No, I could not wish that for her. Remember Lazarus? He experienced death and was brought back, only to have to go through it again. Imagine that! No, I would not want Leticia to have to go through it again.

It turns out the clichés aren't so wrong after all. They fill a void. People don't know what to say to the bereaved. There is an awkwardness surrounding us. Do I mention her or not? Will it cause undue emotions or pain? What do I say? How can I ease the pain? Are there any words that can ease such pain? So we use clichés. And they are right. They are used so often exactly because they are true. Dig past the trite and shallow statement to the truth beneath. Accept them for what they are, a heartfelt attempt at some comfort. A human effort to be sure, but an effort nonetheless.

And so I say, yes, she is indeed in a better place; God knows best; God's will must be done; her task on Earth, as well as her ideas, opinions, and ministry will live on through her legacy. She is with God; she is at peace. She is experiencing joy and love and happiness in the very presence of God himself. It boils down to trust. I trust God. I don't agree with Him, but I trust Him.

A dream of heaven

I have a dream that has been recurring for almost two years now. For almost 24 months, it's been exactly the same. No surprise that I would dream about Leticia; that feeling of loss goes right down into the subconscious. I dream that I can see her in Heaven. She's in the throne room, surrounded by a throng of other worshipers. The walls, which look vaguely like those of a Grecian temple, are transparent, with a golden hue, as if sunlight is streaming through them. The space is vast, and the ceiling, if there is one, is barely discernible far above. In fact, you have this sense that perhaps the temple simply goes on forever.

And there is the throne. It's huge, towering above the people. I'm reminded of the Lincoln Memorial in Washington D.C., except this is more majestic, more awe–inspiring. Like everything else, the throne is slightly transparent, but emits a soft, golden glow. And, of course, on it sits God Himself. I can't see His face; it is lost in the sparkle and glow as I try to look upward.

Everyone is dressed in white robes; the garments also seem to emit a tinge of golden sunray. Thousands of people are thronged before the throne. They are recognizable. Glorified bodies, perhaps, but still the same people they were as mortals. And there is Leticia. No surprise, she's up toward the front, on the right, nearest to the foot of the throne. I can only see the back of her head. But I know it's Leticia.

That's where my dream had always stopped. But last night something different happened, something new. The scene was the same, the action the same. I could still see Leticia toward the front, with thousands of people between us. But this time, as I drew closer, the crowd seemed to draw apart. Not making a line or aisle, but just spreading out so I could have a better view. I walked toward her as the people around me made room. I found myself almost abreast of her, just slightly behind and to the left.

Then she turned her head. She didn't fully turn around, just swiveled a bit from the waist and turned her head toward me. She looked me in the eye and offered her hand, drawing me up next to her. And she smiled at me. Nothing more. No big hug or tears, just a smile and a squeeze of my hand, to say, "I'm glad you are here." Then she turned her face back to God.

I've studied a great deal about Heaven over the course of the last two years. The more I read, the less I understand. The reality is that, for all the books, all the testimonies, all the theories and hypotheses that are out there, we simply don't know. It's all just speculation, mixed with hope, as we try with our limited human capacity to understand something that is beyond us. I don't know how accurate my dream picture is. My own theology of heaven is muddled with my own hopes and desires. But this I do know: Leticia's there, and someday, in some way, she'll welcome me home.

From: **Brian Saunders**
To: **Ivan Wild, Craig Bowler**
Date: **May 14, 2012, 11:01 PM**
Re: **It's the little things …**

Ivan, Craig,

Thought for today: Grief is an unpredictable beast. It's sly and cunning. It comes when you least expect it. Today was one of those days. It came out of the blue. I didn't see it coming. And so I wasn't prepared. Ivan, you were there. In fact it was you and Jennifer who triggered it. Nothing spectacular or deeply emotional. No one said the wrong thing or made a tasteless comment. Just an everyday action—something you didn't think about; you probably didn't even notice. I wouldn't have noticed either; wouldn't have given it a second thought. Except I did. And grief and sorrow and loneliness and isolation all came flooding back.

We were sitting there in the training college dining room having lunch. I was across the table from you, and the seat next to you was empty. Jennifer came up, sat down in the empty chair, reached over and put her arm across yours. Just a normal, simple gesture. Couples do it every day. It's not hugely romantic, nor does it convey deep emotions or intimacy. It's just matter-of-fact. Normal. Mundane. And that's the point. It is anything but mundane. It conveys affection, comfort and security. It's the act of someone who has someone else, of people who are comfortable with each other. It's the normalcy of it that hit me. The fact that this simple gesture of comfort and affection is something that Leticia and I will never experience again. Never. The reminder that she is gone. Forever. So the grief came again. Sorrow, anger, loneliness, isolation, depression, a broken heart. It's all still there. It hit hard and I felt every bit of it. I wanted to slip away, to find someplace to be alone so I could let the emotions out. And then the moment passed. The clouds lifted and I smiled. I'm glad you have each other. And I'm happy for you. I doubt anyone noticed. It sneaks up on me less often these days. I guess that's good. I'm getting stronger, more confident and comfortable with my new life. Yet I know it's always there. Lurking in the shadows, ready to pounce.

Seeking guidance along the path

I have been fortunate, over the past several years, to be able to rely on the counsel and guidance of two trusted friends. I have family, a good support system, and of course, I have God. I've spent hours in prayer seeking His guidance, His succor, His presence. Prayer is entering into a Presence and a peace that passes all understanding. It brings comfort and balm. But it does not always bring answers.

In 2012, I began to recreate the timeline of Leticia's illness. What began as a logistics project became something much deeper as Craig and Ivan and I began a discussion on suffering, grief, and prayer.

From: Brian Saunders
To: Ivan Wild, Craig Bowler
Date: July 8, 2012, 6:18 AM
Re: 3 Years ago today

Just a quick note this morning. I've been doing some research for my paper, collecting the various bulletins and notes about Leticia's illness. It was exactly three years ago today that I sent out the first health bulletin, giving details of her hospitalization and asking for prayer.

brian

From: Craig Bowler
To: Brian Saunders, Ivan Wild
Date: July 8, 2012, 01:17 PM
Re: Re: 3 Years ago today

Brian,

Could we talk about prayer and how you view it now, three years after writing this note?

cb

From: **Brian Saunders**

To: **Craig Bowler, Ivan Wild**

Date: **July 9, 2012, 6:44 AM**

Re: **Re: 3 Years ago today**

I'm not sure my thoughts on prayer have changed, although, like my theology of heaven, they have certainly become more personal and "real." ... I think it all goes back to the age—old question: Why do we pray? What's the point? If God is sovereign, then His will cannot be changed. The Old Testament gives some examples that people use to theorize that God changes His mind when people pray, but those are up for interpretation. And if we are to pray "in God's will," then isn't that just diminishing our request? If we want healing, we pray for healing, but what if that is not God's plan? Then how do we know what to pray? When do we move from praying for healing to praying for a peaceful end? And isn't that in itself a lack of faith? And what difference does it make?

So, I have all the normal thoughts and questions, but they have moved from theory and theology to personal and real. Of course I have the "right" answers—I've said them over and over to others, and I truly believe them. The easy answer is a bit fatalistic: I don't know, but I still trust God. That's fine but it's not very deep. Perhaps it does not need to be. Still, it does make you wonder ...

Brian

From: Ivan Wild

To: Brian Saunders, Craig Bowler

Date: July 9, 2012, 1:52 PM

Re: Re: 3 Years ago today

Thinking back on this time when Leticia first went to the hospital with the stroke. God did answer the prayer. Leticia's memory came fully back; her thoughts, intellect, and memory were intact. In the hospital, though physically declining, her spirit, emotions, thoughts, words, and love were still Leticia. The medical complications did not have dominion over her; she was so at peace with God. It confirmed to me God's presence in her life. My prayers were being answered.

From: Craig Bowler

To: Brian Saunders , Ivan Wild

Date: July 10, 2012, 11:09 AM

Re: Re: 3 Years ago today

I don't think the question is, "Does God answer prayer?" But does He actually do anything with the specifics of the prayer? For example, when I pray that the "doctors' hands would be guided," does that matter to Him? Does it matter if I pray for my kid to have a great roommate in college? Does that change His plan from not having a good roommate?

cb

From: **Brian Saunders**
To: **Craig Bowler , Ivan Wild**
Date: **July 12, 2012, 9:39 PM**
Re: **Re: 3 Years ago today**

We pray because we believe that it does indeed affect the future; that it does alter the course of God's plans. He already knows the outcome—because He already knew of the faith of those in need.

After Leticia told me she was going Home, I didn't pray for healing, or even that it would be an easy death, just that God would protect Holden from bitterness. Earnest and heart—breakingly open prayer. And to be honest, my prayers about me or Leticia were not always very nice to God.

brian

From: **Brian Saunders**
To: **Craig Bowler, Ivan Wild**
Date: **July 13, 2012, 09:14 AM**
Re: **Re: 3 Years ago today**

But the question remains: What effect do my prayers have on the person in the hospital bed? Literally thousands of people across the globe prayed for months for her healing. Was it in vain? Of course not. God was listening; he just said "no." I have to trust in His bigger plan.

From: Craig Bowler

To: Brian Saunders , Ivan Wild

Date: July 13, 2012, 4:46 PM

Re: Re: 3 Years ago today

This is important stuff. As I reread the conversation just now, the first thing that strikes me is how grateful I am to have a safe place to ask these kinds of questions, to have this kind of conversation. I need this space. It helps me "work out my own salvation."

I believe God answers prayer. I believe sometimes He steps in and does something crazy. I also believe sometimes He says, "No." He says, "I'm not going to do anything crazy." And sometimes He says "wait." He says, "Just trust me with this thing." I can hear Him say to me sometimes, "Do you just want my power or do you want my Person?" He whispers, "If I gave you the plan, or the answer you are so desperately seeking, would I then not hear from you for the next six months?" I think there are times when I just want Him to act the way I want Him to act. I want Him to come through for me in a very literal sense. When Jesus says, "Ask anything, and it will be given to you," I literally want that to happen.
 I'm learning that God wants me to trust the Healer more than the healing. It's always the heart that He's after. So whether it's anger or gossip, self–sufficiency or pride, or celiac disease, the Healer is always most interested in my heart. He wants me to hold His hand, and pray for all things, recognizing that He knows best and He will prevail and He will ultimately resolve the situation.

He's the "author and perfecter" of my faith, and I have to re-member that. When I look for Him to make my circumstances better, I miss the benefit of moving through those challenging seasons with the Healer. I need the process of healing, or learning or growing, more than I need the outcome. The final outcome is on the other side, and most days I'm OK with that. I think this might be sounding fatalistic, but that's not how I'm feeling. I'm seeing a resolution; just not here.

Oh, one more thing about healing. I've decided that more than anything else, God uses people to heal people. He's answering my prayers by healing me, and He is doing that through you guys. So thanks.

Echoes in the valley

"

We are called to devote our lives to
the people God has placed within our
care—to pastor them, shepherd them,
nurture and care for them.

"

NINE

Leticia's legacy

For anyone who has lost someone, legacy becomes an important component of keeping the person alive—through the actions, attitudes, and beliefs of the one who is gone. She creates a legacy by living on in the lives of others. A legacy is like the echo of a voice; it may not be a loud voice, but the echoes continue to resound long after the voice has been silenced. Even a small voice can have a lasting effect. It's how we know she mattered. It's why God put her on this Earth.

It has become important to me to establish Leticia's legacy. In so doing, I ensure that her influence, if not her life, will carry on. I have come to champion her causes and, even in cases where I disagreed with her, I argue her side of an issue. I find myself teaching things she taught me.

From: Brian Saunders
To: Craig Bowler, Ivan Wild
Date: September 17, 2012, 12:15 AM
Re: Legacy and Letting go...

With a distance of three years, the immediacy of Leticia's loss begins to fade in the eyes of the world. She becomes an impersonal memory to everyone else. Add to that the fact that, the more time passes, the more my life includes people who have never met Leticia, and who see me, not as half of the couple "BrianandLeticia," but as simply "Brian." So my emotions need a sense of that connection. I'm sure it is simply part of the cycle. As we enter into this "season of milestones" each year, my thoughts turn more and more to Leticia. So, in sharing them with you, it's just a means of including you in my thoughts and memories—and making sure someone else remembers.

brian

From: Brian Saunders
To: Craig Bowler, Ivan Wild
Date: September 22, 2012, 06:05 AM
Re: Re: Legacy and letting go...

I'm sure there are deeper reasons why I am drawn back to this timeline of three years ago. It has something to do with the widening gap of time between Leticia and me. I am afraid of

NOT missing her. It's a feeling that if I don't keep her memory close, I will lose it. I know her memory and influence will fade in everyone else's consciousness, and that's OK. It's normal and expected. But it should not be so with me. I cannot picture the long term without Leticia, yet, as time progresses, it is becoming a reality. Seventeen years from now, I will have been apart from her as long as I knew her. I can do the day−to−day. It's the long term that I struggle with. It is hard to imagine. And I still don't like the idea of people knowing me as an individual and not as part of a couple.

I'm still coming to grips with the fact that the rest of the world will soon enough forget her, but of course, I will not. I understand that those who knew her will not really forget her, but with time, her influence lessens, and the memories of her fade. That is the normal course of things. I suppose that is why we have memorials and sayings 11 years after 9/11: "We will never forget," so that people don't let the loss fade into insignificance.

I talked with a retired officer at a funeral in Oregon on Wednesday. His wife was "promoted to Glory" six months ago. This was the first funeral he felt strong enough to attend. Tears in his eyes, he said simply, "I know you understand." Yeah, I get it. I remember those hot, piercing moments of grief. I still get them.

So I'll keep her memories close and keep looking backward, even as I look ahead. I'm learning that this is who I am now.

brian

From: **Brian Saunders**

To: **Craig Bowler, Ivan Wild**

Date: **November 4, 2012, 5:46 AM**

Re: **Re: Legacy and letting go …**

Still processing the timeline of three years ago. This is my analytical self, self—analyzing my own analysis. (Yup, say that fast three times.) For the past three years, I have been focusing on my own grief and loss. I have not really con-sidered what Leticia was going through. At the time I was both too busy and too naive to understand what she was dealing with during the months before her death. I was just trying to keep everything together. Once in a while, of course, her frustrations would come out, particularly when she could no longer walk, and the therapists did not seem helpful. (That's why she devised her own exercise routine using her cane.) But for the most part, she was content, positive, and hopeful.

But I've been thinking about the timeline. She was in the hospital for so long. Today is November 4. Do you remem-ber August 1 of this year? How long ago does it seem? Think about all the stuff you've done since the beginning of August—all the activities you have participated in, all the places you have gone, and the milestones that have occurred. Three years ago at this time, Leticia had been in the hospital since August. And, although she did not know it, as of this day, she had five more weeks to go. She was in the hospital on Holden's first day of high school. She missed band concerts and robotics competitions, Officers

Councils, the fall and Christmas programs at the corps, and so much more.

I guess we all got used to it. It was simply our routine. Drop Holden off at school, go to the hospital for a couple of hours, go to work, pick Holden up at school, go back to the hospital for the afternoon/dinner, go back to the corps for programs or stay at the hospital for the evening, then home to bed. Every day for four months. But she was alone every night in the hospital. She was busy during the day, and of course, she made friends with the doctors, nurses, and staff, but still, she was alone every night for the last four months of her life. It hurts now to think of that. I was too busy to think of it then; now it's coming back. I'm just so sorry she had to endure all that. I'm not beating myself up over it, nor am I falling into some kind of guilt; I just think, now, with time and space, I have a chance to appreciate what she was going through. And I love and respect her all the more for it. She lay in that hospital bed for four months. But she endured it, and she did it with abiding joy and faith. And all of that suffering does not matter now that she is in the presence of God.

brian

From: Craig Bowler
To: Brian Saunders, Ivan Wild
Date: November 6, 2012, 10:36 AM
Re: Re: Legacy and letting go ...

Thanks for sending your thoughts this way. I've been reflecting on this season for you guys and especially Leticia. I'd not thought too much about her pain. It's one of the things I think I try to avoid. I don't like thinking that people are actually suffering. It's easier to make an illustration out of pain, or tell a story about pain, than it is to really think about the actual pain Leticia must have faced. When I do think about this stuff, I think about God's desire to free us from such pain, and at times, to let the pain remain longer than we'd like but to always be on the cusp of healing and freedom until He finally does bring peace and wholeness. For Leticia, her healing came on the other side of life, and now your life is filled with pain—a different kind of pain, but one that is truly very heavy. My prayer is that God will continue to heal you of your pain, strengthen you to share your pain, and allow Him to continue to enter in and give you life in the midst of pain.

cb

From: **Brian Saunders**
To: **Craig Bowler, Ivan Wild**
Date: **November 19, 2012, 7:57**
Re: **Random Thoughts**

Thinking again of three years ago today. By now I was running the Christmas efforts on top of everything else, so it was a very busy time. Keeping busy and staying focused on task meant I did not have to explore my deeper thoughts or contemplate the "what ifs." Of course, even at that point, I was completely optimistic. We had built the ramp for the front door of the house and moved Leticia's office to the dining room. I even put up new window blinds and window tinting with the expectation that she would be spending more time at home during the sunny days. Still, this was really the beginning of the end as, despite her good spirits, the setbacks began to outnumber the advances.

We passed another milestone the other morning: Holden's first attempt at shaving. As a low–key guy, I think this would ordinarily have passed without much thought for me, but since Leticia's death, I have become much more aware. His "peachfuzz" has been growing for months. We've been commenting that we would eventually have to do something about it. So this was the day I taught him to shave. Something that normally I would have shared with Leticia: a guy's rite of passage, a little seemingly insignificant activity that somehow adds more cement to the bond between father and son. I would have just mentioned it casually, and she would have done the mom thing; her eyes would have moistened and she would have expressed those mixed emotions that come with parental milestones: pride in watching her son grow up mingled with melancholy that it is happening so fast. So I suppose that's my job now. Only there is no spouse to share it with. So glad you guys are listening. So yeah, the eyes misted up a bit and the words choked up for a moment, but then it passed. I don't think Holden noticed, but he did realize that here is another milestone passed without Mom. These milestones are not sad occasions; each one is something to be celebrated; they just come now with a slight edge to the joy.

I find that I am bringing up Leticia's name more in class and conversation than I did a year ago. Part of that is simply getting more comfortable with my own thoughts and memories; it is less painful to think of her. Part of it is recognizing that she does indeed still have a lot to offer cadets. In teaching homiletics, I have only my own ministry to use an example; and in my life, "my" ministry has also been hers. So when I talk about sermon calendars and series, about good sermon techniques, etc., I naturally use her as a reference. Many sidebar or "soapbox" comments also come from her mind; the principles that she held have now become my own. There is this abiding need to keep her close in memory and thought. In my recent reading, I've learned that it's all about balance and time—time to heal, to grow more comfortable, to find coping mechanisms, and to find a natural balance between forgetting and oversharing. I trust that you will let me know if I get awkward!

As always, it is the writing and the conversations that are

the real coping mechanism. Who needs a therapist as long as you guys are around. Just don't start charging!

Brian

From:	**Ivan Wild**
To:	**Brian Saunders, Craig Bowler**
Date:	**December 1, 2012, 09:40 AM**
Re:	**Re: Random Thoughts**

You asked about how much you should talk about Leticia. Don't worry about what others may think. Those who are close to you know that you are stable and healthy. You are in a position of teaching and leading; we can only teach from our personal experience. Leticia is a part of that experience, a part of you. It is natural that you speak of her often. After all, you were with her half your life. There has not been much time for you to experience "individual" ministry since Leticia's death, but maybe over time as you have more personal experiences as a single dad and single officer, you will teach and lead more from that perspective. I think you will always refer to Leticia, and rightly so, but milestones like Holden shaving for the first time will come into your teaching and preaching. Continue to share with people the things Leticia taught you and the people she ministered to. Maybe you should write a book so the lessons learned from a wonderful Christian woman will be passed on to further generations. I would buy it, if I get royalties for the idea.

ivan

From: **Brian Saunders**
To: **Craig Bowler, Ivan Wild**
Date: **December 12, 2012, 09:25 AM**
Re: **Wondering**

Today marks the anniversary of that last conversation with Leticia. Last night Holden and I decorated our Christmas trees. There are some traditions we can still do: Pizza Hut, Diet Coke, and two trees: Letica's thematic, white–lights–only, color–coordinated tree in the living room, and another tree with multi–colored lights and all the mismatched family and travel ornaments in the family room. But I couldn't sleep last night. At first I could not figure out why, then I realized that I had had the conversation with Leticia starting around 11 p.m. Add the three hours' time difference—it was 2 a.m. here—and it was exactly three years to the hour of our final talk. God was letting me have a few moments alone with my memories. ...

brian

From: **Brian Saunders/CC/USW/SArmy**
To: **Undisclosed Recipients**
Date: **December 14, 2012, 1:19 PM**
Re: **3 Years**

Dear Friends,

With the advent of Facebook, writing a Christmas newsletter seems redundant. However, on this, the third anniversary of

Leticia's journey Home, it seemed appropriate to share a bit more about our own journey over the past 36 months.

Three years ago today, at 3:40 p.m. Hawaiian time, Holden and I held Leticia's hands as she was released from the bonds of this Earth and ushered into the presence of God. With the perspective of time, I look back and have a sense of the deep sacredness of those moments. Just the three of us, sharing in those last minutes as a family. A heart—wrenching day, but there was a sense of God's presence, and an assurance that she was already Home. Tonight, some very dear friends will be with Holden and me—a different kind of family, but family to be sure. We are blessed to be surrounded by such loving people who continue to walk through life with us.

In true homiletical fashion, let's do this in three sections: Holden, Healing, and Hope....

Holden

Three years ago, Holden was 14, a young teenager, still a boy. Over these past three years I have seen him grow (yes, he's taller than me now although really, that's not saying much!) into a maturing, sincere, faithful young man. I was astounded to see his senior pictures the other day—who was this handsome young man staring back at me through Leticia's eyes? (Happily, Holden gets his looks from Mom.) Undoubtedly, Holden has endured some stresses that kids just should not have to deal with; he has walked this valley alongside me where children should not have to tread. But he has done so with faith and maturity, growing up before my eyes. I saw it first in the hospital—from the first day, when it seemed routine, like so many previous trips to the hospital, to spending every afternoon for four—plus months sitting in Leticia's hospital room, to the day he took over monitoring her heartbeat on the day she died. In June, he will turn 18 and graduate from high school.

Three years ago, on December 11, I had my final conversation alone with Leticia. We knew it would be our last, and she reminded me that it was my duty to watch over Holden's faith and life, to protect him through the challenges that he would face after her death. Her directive was simple: "Deliver Holden into manhood with his faith intact." I'm very pleased to say that Holden continues to walk in faith and confidence.

For as long as I can remember, Holden has wanted to fly. I recall pushing him on the swings when he was 3 or 4 while he sang a song of his own creation: "I want to fly high; I want to touch the sky." Three years and two days ago, during that last conversation with Mom, she encouraged him never to give up on his dream. Fittingly, two days ago, exactly three years after that conversation, Holden flew solo for the first time. It was a powerful moment as I watched him take off (and a much better moment 90 minutes later when I watched him land!).

Healing

The loss of a loved one has been described as a wound, a tear in the flesh that not only causes extreme pain but lays one open to infection—bitterness, anger, remorse, and depression. Thankfully, a wound can heal. Although it will leave a scar, the tear will eventually close over.

For me, healing comes through friends, ministry, and legacy. I have been blessed by many amazing, faithful friends who have journeyed with me along this path. Ivan, Craig, and I share a bond deeper than I can describe. They have supported me every step of the way along this path. Dave, Dusty, and others have been constant in pastoral care and friendship, and I am deeply appreciative of all they have done. My ministry—both in Honolulu and now at the training college—has also been part of the healing process. I am blessed with a work that God has called me to, a work that I enjoy immensely. Finally, and perhaps most importantly, I see Leticia's legacy all around me. People continue to remind me how Leticia blessed them, taught them, encouraged them, or guided them. Here at the training college, I have the privilege of interacting frequently with young officers like Megan and Arwyn, who trace the spiritual lineage of their calling back to Leticia's influence.

So the healing comes. Putting it back into the journey allegory, I would say we began with baby steps and then learned to walk again. We are now traveling along with a degree of confidence, missing our companion, but knowing that we can journey on. We even jog sometimes!

Hope
And of course, hope remains. Not the Christmas—morning—I'm—hoping—for—a—bike kind of hope, but biblical hope, the anticipation of a known outcome. We know our family will be whole again, and that not only will the wound be healed, but even the scar will also be erased. This journey will end, and a new one will begin. ...

So, not exactly a Christmas letter, but it brings you up to date with us. Now, as Christmas approaches, our thoughts turn to that greatest hope of all: Christ himself, God Incarnate, coming for the salvation of the world. May Christ's coming be just as real in your heart as it was in Bethlehem all those years ago.

Brian

Recently I had plaques made for each member of my staff at the training college that share something Leticia told me long ago. One day, I was busy and frustrated with all the people who kept coming into my office with questions and concerns. I was so busy with all these "interruptions" that I was not getting my "real" work done. "The interruptions ARE the job," Leticia said. People matter. In ministry, as in life, it is the people around us who really count. The paperwork and deadlines can wait, but people deserve our care and attention. I took her lesson to heart that day and have strived to live by it ever since. So, I embossed her admonition onto cardstock and put it into frames for the staff. And Leticia's legacy—the echoes of her voice—continue to resound.

I often repeat Leticia's stance on family and priorities: "Family is the only congregation you take with you," she would say. A good point. As Salvation Army officers, we move from assignment to assignment, changing jobs and leaving congregations behind in our wake. We are called to devote our lives to the people God has placed within our care—to pastor them, shepherd them, nurture and care for them. We spend all our time focused on others. Yet when we leave, the only people who go with us are our families. Our families are the only people we continue to be responsible for, year in and year out, regardless of location or appointment. What good is it if I save the entire city, yet lose my own kid? Yes, our families need to be our priority; we must not only minister *with* them, but minister *to* them as well. Another echo of that voice.

From:	**Brian Saunders**
To:	**CC Cadets**
Date:	**December 17, 2012, 08:49 AM**
Re:	**Legacy**

Dear Cadets,

As some of you may know, Friday was the third anniversary of my wife Leticia's death. I suppose it will always be a difficult day, but on this particular evening, I was blessed to be surrounded by close friends, sessionmates, and lifelong companions who have been on this journey with Leticia and me since the beginning. I've been thinking about legacy a great deal over the weekend. Legacy is, according to the dictionary, "that which is left behind." It is the impression or influence we leave upon people. It's about the impact we have made on people's lives, and how we may have influenced or even changed the course of their lives through our interactions and relationships.

I've been thinking about Leticia's legacy—that which she left behind. It can be seen in the lives of the many people with whom and to whom she ministered. As an officer, she touched thousands of lives, some with just a bag of toys at Christmas, others with a deep relationship that grew through years of discipleship and mentoring. Yesterday I noticed a greeting card taped to the inside cover of one of Leticia's Bibles. It is dated November 3, 1991, a month before we were married, when Leticia was the assistant officer at Pasadena Tabernacle. It begins, "Dear Lt. Adams, I cannot begin to express my gratitude for the love you shared with me the other night. What we shared defies description, and I thank God, as it could only be a most precious and perfectly timed gift from Him." The note concludes with these words, "I can't remember anything quite as wonderful as being held by you and prayed for by you. You even wiped away my tears. You have helped me make it when I might not have otherwise. You made me feel loved." Leticia wrote a note to herself on the leaf of the Bible just beneath the card: "Let this card always serve as a reminder as to what the ministry is, and what I have been called for."

Cadets, as you head into your final week of your Christmas ministry, remember what you have been called for. Show up; be holy. Do the work. Love the people. I trust you will leave a positive legacy. I pray that you will leave an indelible impression upon those you have served and those with whom you have ministered. I trust your legacy will be one of hard work and commitment, of dedication and of servants' hearts. Mostly, I pray that it will be about love and care for those around you. Finish well.

My prayer for you today is from Hebrews, Chapter 13: "May the God of peace, who through the blood of the eternal covenant brought back from the dead our Lord Jesus, that great shepherd of the sheep, equip you with everything good for doing his will, and may he work in us what is pleasing to him, through Jesus Christ, to whom be glory for ever and ever." blessings

Major Saunders

Leticia's greatest legacy, the greatest testament to her ministry, is in the lives of the people she touched. Her ministry was built around personal relationships—young women she counseled, mentored, and shared with. While there have been many, three stand out. All three are Salvation Army officers.

Tracy was a young Salvationist at our corps in Dunstable, England. She wanted to be an officer, but struggled with feelings of unworthiness. Leticia's counsel was always: "God has called you. He will equip you."

Megan is an officer serving in the USA Western Territory. She was a college student attending our corps when we lived in Salem, Oregon. Leticia built a relationship with her as her mentor and pastor. Megan thought God might be calling her into full-time ministry but was unsure and afraid. Megan and Leticia talked and prayed about it. After we were transferred away from Oregon, they stayed in touch, communicating frequently over the years. In Megan's words:

> Major Leticia was always praying with me, guiding me, answering my questions, and showing me an unwavering joy and faith in Christ. With Major Leticia's help, I was able to see and accept that God had called me to officership. Though I tried to fight it, giving Major Leticia all sorts of reasons why I shouldn't, she always had very logical and biblical reasons why I should. Finally, I made the decision. I know that it was God who called me, and I am the one who accepted, but it was Major Leticia who helped to guide my heart and mind in the right direction.

In July of 2009, Leticia wrote to Megan one last time. She told her that she was sure of God's calling for her life. "Accept, follow it. You'll never be sorry," she wrote. As it turns out, it was the last email Leticia ever wrote. Fitting. Another echo.

Arwyn is another young lady Leticia had the privilege of ministering to while we were stationed in Honolulu. When she was a cadet, she shared this testimony:

> When I accepted my calling to journey with The Salvation Army and become a soldier, Major Leticia Saunders, my corps officer and mentor, gave me a verse: "Take delight in the Lord, and he will give you the desires of your heart." (Psalm 37:4) I saw it at the time as an affirmation. If I continued on in my path of sanctification, God would bring my hopes to fruition. A year and a half later I was sitting at my beloved officer's memorial service. I didn't know how to handle

the death of the person I wanted to be when I grew up. I didn't know how to hope when all I saw was pain and fear creeping back in. She was the best example of a life led by a confident hope in Jesus Christ. I looked down at the program and saw her picture with her life verse: Psalm 37:4. I didn't know until that moment that she had given me her own favorite verse when I stepped out in hope. In her darkest moments she defied fear and embraced the hope of Jesus. Her hope in the Lord led many others—including me—to put their hope in the Lord. The desire of her heart was the Lord, and for Him, she gave everything. I knew what I had to be when I grew up. I needed to love the Lord and only the Lord, for he is my true desire. My righteousness is as filthy rags compared to delighting in Him. I need to confidently rest all my hope in Him and never look back.

"My hope is built on nothing less than Jesus love and righteousness." (*On Christ the Solid Rock I Stand*) I don't need to live in fear. I don't need to concern myself with things that are too big for me to understand. My hope is in Jesus. Like Major Leticia, my delight is in the Lord.

Another echo. Legacy indeed.

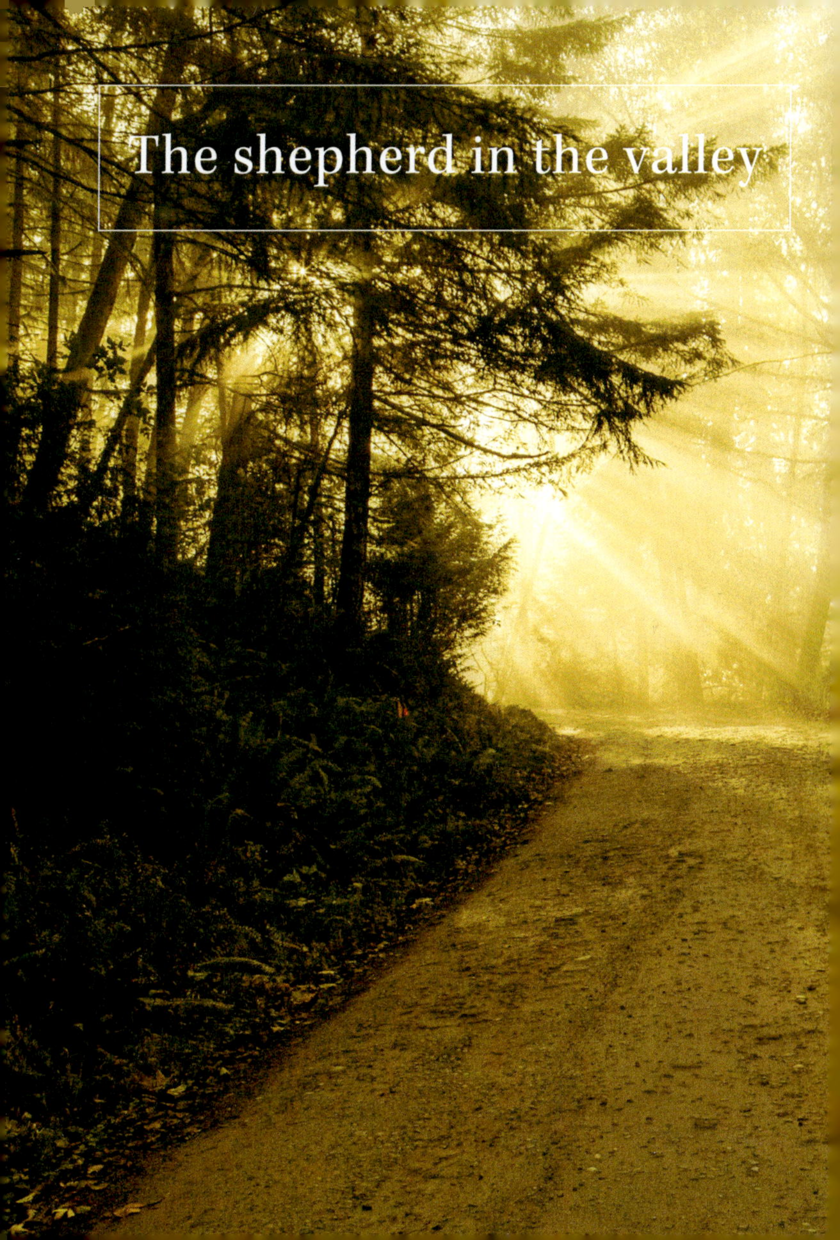
The shepherd in the valley

> Grief can trap you, hold you down, make
> you feel as if you can never take another
> step. So I choose to keep moving forward.
> One step at a time.

TEN

AS I HAVE WALKED THROUGH this "valley of the shadow of death," God has been my Shepherd. He has been my provider and counselor, my guide and my companion. True, I have benefited from friends and family, from many helping hands and willing hearts, but it has been God who has carried me through.

I have been walking through this valley for several years now. The hurt has been real, the scars deep, the pain visceral. I have wept, yelled, pouted, cursed, complained, and bargained. I have had to watch my son grow up without his mother. My world collapsed, and I have had to redefine myself, shaping a whole new future out of the ruins of what once seemed so solid. And yet, through it all, I've been able to rely on this inner confidence, this inner peace, that can come only from God. Honestly, if it's been this hard for me, I cannot fathom how hard it must be for those without hope in the resurrection.

Cliché as it is, I KNOW that I will be reunited with Leticia someday, and I've come to understand that God truly does work all things together for the good of those who love Him. This "good" is not an earthly happiness kind of good, but an eternal, redemptive good. Whatever God's purpose for allowing this valley in my life, I know I can trust Him because He is walking through it right alongside me.

This Shepherd knows all the paths, all the hills and vales. He knows when I need extra light or additional supplies. He nudges me in the right direction and keeps watch over my shoulder as I pause for refreshment. As long as I keep moving forward, He supplies what I need. The Bible reminds us that Jesus is the Light of the World, and that His Word is a lamp for our feet. These lights provide illumination for me as I walk through this valley. His presence and His Word point the way before me.

Psalm 23:1 declares, "The Lord is my shepherd, I lack nothing." It's a testament to God's providence, a statement of faith. This valley can be cruel. The terrain is often treacherous; the conditions unsettled. It's hard going. Yet this witness rings true. God knows our thoughts and our feelings. He knows our hurts and our anguish. He knows what we need—even when we don't. And so we claim with the Psalmist: "I lack nothing." As long as He is near, I have all I need.

The comforting words of verses two and three speak deeply to this need: "He makes me lie down in green pastures, he leads me beside quiet waters, he refreshes my soul." A green pasture, a quiet brook. Safety, sustenance, security. A place of peace and assurance. Out there, in the middle of this harsh, unforgiving terrain, is an oasis. A place that God brings us to restore our souls. A place of healing. A place of rest.

As I look back over the years since Leticia died, I see those pastures here and there. Throughout this valley God has brought me over and over again to places of quiet restoration: the echo of Leticia's voice in the chapel, the delight in finding her handwriting in that officer address book, wise words spoken by friends and pastors. They remind me that Leticia is still part of me and that, more important, that God is still here as well. Providing moments, blessings, and yes, a future.

The heart of Psalm 23 is verse four: "Even though I walk through the darkest valley, I will fear no evil, for you are with me." Here, in this dark place, God abides. The Shepherd does not abandon His sheep, but walks right alongside me, protecting, guiding. It is His presence that provides comfort and sustenance. It is His presence that provides restoration and peace. He is with me as I walk.

The walking itself is important. It suggests movement, progress. Although those oases are good, the reality is I cannot stay there. The journey continues. The rest stop experiences are meant to be just that, moments of restoration and joy that sustain and encourage me as I travel along. Grief can trap you, hold you down, make you feel as if you can never take another step. So I choose to keep moving forward. One step at a time. I keep breathing, keep stumbling along. Eventually, I am able to look back and notice I am not stumbling anymore. I am walking, sometimes even running. I am no longer afraid of the future; I am able to see the positives in life, to enjoy the moments and milestones. Because God is with me.

And then David, the Psalmist, makes this last statement: "Surely goodness and mercy will follow me all the days of my life, and I will dwell in the house of the Lord forever." (Psalm 23:6) In the darkest recesses of the valley, where no light seems to penetrate the dense forest and rocky crags, it is sometimes difficult to see this "goodness and mercy." That's when I have cried out to God: "Where's all that goodness now, God?" And yet it is there, right there in the darkest recesses of my hurt and pain. David's psalm is one of faith.

Even though I am going through this agony, I can know that God's love and protection are here. I feel it; I draw strength from it. I know there is still good out there; I am still capable of joy and happiness. I simply need to trust. I trust in that final promise, the one that dries every tear and erases every sorrow: "...and I will dwell in the house of the Lord forever."

POSTSCRIPT

Dearest Reader,

Thank you for coming along on this journey with me. If you have made it this far, you have my heartfelt gratitude and appreciation for putting up with more than three years of angst and analysis. Thank you for wading through personal letters and random thoughts. I am more grateful than you can possibly know.

You may recall, if you read the preface, that this book is not for you. It is not written for any particular demographic, nor is it designed to teach about grief or train in counseling. It is simply one man's journey through the valley of grief. I wrote it for me—but perhaps something resonated with you. Maybe it has helped you to understand something a bit differently or to consider something in a new light. Perhaps these reflections have reminded you of your own thoughts and feelings as you traveled a similar path; after all, valleys are a part of everyone's journey.

I met with Ivan and Craig again the other day. The topic was this book. "Hey, when are you going to finish it?" they chided. After all, it had been "done" for months. I'd been tweaking and fiddling with it. "Get it done already!" was the challenge.

Then, "Why *haven't* you finished it?" A much deeper question indeed.

"I don't have a conclusion yet."

"Are you waiting for one?"

And there was the heart of the matter. I had not finished the writing because I was simply not ready to. I revised and amended, continuing to refine and adjust bits and pieces. But really, I was simply not ready to close the book. I was not ready to end this chapter in my life. This writing had been a connection to Leticia, an excuse to remain in my memories. It had been my balm and my therapy. I was not ready for it to end.

I realized that I had been waiting for a "conclusion," some defining moment or event or some dawning recognition that would signify that I had emerged from the valley into the Promised Land. Had "acceptance" come and gone, and I missed it? Worse, had I not "arrived" there yet?

The truth is that there is no conclusion. I wrote three years ago about a dream in which I realized that I would be in this valley for a long time. "Somehow, I know I will be on this path the rest of my life. This is a permanent journey, a walk that will never cease." And that's it. There is no conclusion, no end. A conclusion cannot be written because there is none in life.

But this writing must draw to a close. Although there is no closure to be found, no particular milestone or event that signifies, "Now it's finished." There is no end to this valley. That's OK. Its not about the terrain, it's about how you choose to traverse it and with whom you travel. The valley is my "forever normal." And I'm comfortable walking *in* it. Not "through" it—implying there is an exit or an end—but in it, knowing that I am not alone, knowing that there is light and peace and joy and friendship and laughter there.

So I had to choose a time, a day, a moment, and be done. This is the day. I've come a long way. The path behind me already grows dim. I can look behind or ahead; the trail winds its way through the valley as far as the eye can see. There is nothing special to mark this day—no epiphany or realization. No singular moment or milestone. Just an ordinary Sunday afternoon.

The journey continues. The path continues to wind its way through the valley. Sometimes the mountains on either side are steep, tall, and foreboding; other times they are more like gentle, rolling hills. Sometimes it seems dark; other times, it's bright and sunny. Holden and I walk it without Leticia, but she is never far from us. She will always be a part of us. Our story will unfold and our journey continue through this life and into the next, where it will play out for all eternity. And God is here. We walk on.

> *"Even though I walk through the valley*
> *of the shadow of death,*
> *I will fear no evil, for You are with me."*

Psalm 23:4 (NIV 1984)

Epilogue

August 8, 2013

Dear Leticia,

Today was the day! The day Holden passed his check ride and became a licensed pilot. He's accomplished something spectacular; achieved such an amazing goal. I'm so proud of him. Today was a day like no other. A day we have all been looking forward to for such a long time, a day that I know you so much wanted to see. And I can't express how deeply I wish you were here to see it.

Remember when Holden was a toddler in Portland? We took him to the park just down the block from our house to swing on the swing set. And he made up that song: "I wanna go high; I wanna touch the sky." Even at that young age, he wanted to swing higher and higher; he wanted to be in the sky. A dream was born.

He took every opportunity to fly: tourist flights, young pilot clubs; he was even allowed into the cockpits of commercial planes after 9/11. In Guam, at age 11, he made his choice: "I want to be a pilot." That was it.

I'll never forget that last conversation with you. Holden and I held your hands as you shared and blessed us. You told him you wanted him to pursue his dream and not stop until it was accomplished. Three years later, he's done it.

I so wish you could have seen him these last three years. As soon as we moved to L.A., he looked into the Flight School at Torrance Airport and started taking lessons. We purchased the manuals and arranged with his instructor to start working systematically through the lessons. He stayed up late and woke up early. Some months flying took a backseat, but slowly but surely, he built up his hours and worked through the lessons. He passed his first stage check and, just before Christmas, he made his first solo flight.

It's hard to describe what it's like to watch our son take off. I stood on the edge of the runway as his instructor, Brandon, went up with Holden through a couple of "touch and go's." Then they taxied off the runway, and Brandon got out. Holden was on his own. He taxied, was cleared, and made his way down the runway, building speed. Within a few seconds, he was off the ground, and I watched as our son took flight, in sole command of a plane for the first time. He climbed, then banked into a right turn, heading back past the airport. I could still see the plane; it was just a speck in the sky, and I thought, Wow, that's my son up there.

After that, lots more hours, lots more lessons in preparation for "the day."

And every chance I got, I went down to the airport to watch him take off. Often I would just leave the office, drive to the airport, walk directly onto the runway, and stay just long enough to watch the take-off before heading back. Other times, the flight school would give me the radio and a golf cart. Other people watch their kids' soccer games; I watch mine fly a plane. So cool.

This week was the pinnacle. He did his oral test and flight stage check and passed fine. He took several practice written tests and worked on the flight plan for today. On Wednesday he did his last practice maneuvers with Brandon. And today, starting at 10 a.m., he began the final tests. The written exam was first, lasting about two hours, followed by the oral test. Finally, at about 1, they went up for his actual check ride. I was in a seminar at the training college, but by about 2, I couldn't take it anymore and headed to the airport. Richard and May, the owners of the flight school, along with a couple of other pilots, waited with me. Finally, at about 4 p.m., Holden texted me. "Passed. Come to the airport." I texted back, "I'm already here."

I knew I would cry. I shed tears the day he took that first solo. I've held them back on any number of occasions as I stood alone on the runway watching that speck in the sky that was Holden. All along, every step of the way, I knew this is what you wanted to see. And I ache that you have missed it. This is one of those irreplaceable milestones of his life. Something never to be repeated. Something that his mom should have been there for. My tears were of joy and pride but also of sorrow, deep grief and pain—knowing that you can't see this.

There is something about watching Holden fly that touches my heart. It's more than just a dad's pride in his son's incredible achievement. Somehow, because of that last conversation with you, his flying is connected to your legacy, your memory. I see you when I watch him fly; I remember your encouragement and support for his dream; and I can hear your voice urging him to see it through.

When I watch Holden fly, somehow, I feel like he is closer to you. Now, I know that's not theologically correct, but I'm sure you'll forgive me this one theological indiscretion. Maybe it's because he is up in the air, up in the sky, in the place we imagine "Heaven" to be. Maybe it's because you were so instrumental in motivating him to follow this path. I sometimes can almost picture you—a semitransparent version of you—floating outside the plane, reaching in and caressing his cheek as he flies. Corny, I know, but somehow, it comforts me to think of you being up there with him. It feels like he is closer to you when he flies.

For the past year, I have told Holden that I planned to be his first passenger. I don't often go up with him and Brandon, but I assured him that I wanted to be the first person he took up once he got his license. Ten minutes after he passed the test, I got my wish. The FAA examiner printed out his temporary license; they both signed it; she signed his log book; and Richard simply told Holden, "The plane is yours. Take your dad up." So up we went. I sat in the front seat next to him. I was so proud and pleased and excited and thrilled for him that I never thought of being nervous. Of course he has my full confidence. I tried to take some pictures—we just flew the practice pattern up over Long Beach harbor, along the coast to Rancho Palos Verdes and over our house. The view below was nice, but the view next to me was even better. Imagine that, sitting next to your son as he pilots a plane. Trust and faith like nothing else! All too soon we headed back. At dinner tonight he mentioned how he could feel the stress and adrenaline bleeding away. I told him that it was a good day indeed, a day to be proud. I told him that I was proud of him and you were too. That's all I needed to say. He knows.

So that was today. We missed you. But you were here. You always will be. Love you.

MAJOR BRIAN SAUNDERS is a fifth-generation Salvation Army officer, currently serving as the Training Principal at the College for Officer Training in the USA Western Territory. As the son of officer parents, Brian grew up in various cities in the western and central United States as well as the Caribbean. He attended Azusa Pacific University as a pre-law student where he received a bachelor's degree in political science. Heeding God's call, he resigned from Law School and headed instead to The Salvation Army's School for Officer's Training, where he graduated and was commissioned as an officer with the "Servants of Jesus" session in 1991.

Brian and Leticia met as cadets and were married soon after training. Their first appointment was back to the training school, during which time their son Holden was born. After five years at the school, there followed a number of corps and training appointments including assignments to locations as varied as England and Guam.

Leticia passed away due to complications from pneumonia in 2009 while they were stationed in Honolulu, Hawaii. While Brian and Holden continue to miss Leticia, they rejoice in the knowledge that she is celebrating in the eternal presence of God.

Brian holds a master's degree in theology and a doctorate of ministry degree in clergy education, both from Fuller Theological Seminary.

Brian and Leticia's son, Holden, attends Embry-Riddle Aeronautical University where he is studying aeronautical science.

FRONTIER PRESS

THE SALVATION ARMY USA WESTERN TERRITORY

Visit frontierpress.org to download a free digital copy of this book and others published by The Salvation Army USA Western Territory.